the
MYSTERY
of
MAN

An Anthropologic Study

by

Owen Sharkey

Franklin Publishing Company
2047 Locust Street
Philadelphia, Pa. 19103

Preface

This *Theological Anthropology* is written within the framework of an existential Ontology. It seeks to be illuminating within each man's experience of life and his self-understanding. At the same time it considers man's self-understanding within the framework of the whole of reality. It perceives this whole to be a dynamic play of opposites or contraries. It implies that what is stated as intelligible can be experienced by each man. One should be able to realize the correct meaning existentially.

In my experience and self-understanding I seek to find myself. From such a viewpoint, an existential Ontology brings one to *Anthropology*. And if man is embodied *spirit*, the question must be placed: What grounds man's spirit? This brings one to a *Theological Anthropology*. This general perspective is set forth in the *Introduction*. The *method* followed is indicated. It is one of self-understanding, experiencing the intelligibility of the whole of reality. Using such a method, I am not seeking to prove anything by rational argument. I seek, rather, to indicate the phenomena associated with human self-awareness. The phenomena experienced tend to indicate the deeper reality.

Chapter One considers the *Problematic of Man*. Man is a mystery and a problem to himself. He is forever questioning himself. His questions arise out of a play of opposites. They cover every facet of his life. Answers, to the extent that one perceives or finds answers to his questions, are always given within man himself. They are given with a perceived meaning or intelligibility.

The Problematic of Man always remains as long as we live. Obviously, then, the Problematic remains throughout this book. I would be extremely foolish to think that I had dissolved the problem. Yet, at the same time, man out of his self-awareness and understanding does tend to answer the questions placed before him from various viewpoints. Hence:

Chapter Two considers *Philosophical Anthropology*, or how man tends to answer the mystery of himself through intellectual insights.

iii

Chapter Three considers *Theological Anthropology*, or how man tends to answer out of his religious awareness and self-understanding.

Chapter Four considers *Man as an Historical Reality*. Man tends to answer the problems and questions placed before him in the context of space and time. His imaged ideas are always associated with life experienced in this world.

Chapter Five presents *The Hebrew and Christian Conception of Man*. Both Hebrew and Christian answers are given within an historical understanding of reality. *Chapter Six and Chapter Seven* belong with this framework of understanding. Obviously to a Jew and Christian man is a *Unit of Matter and Spirit* (Chapter Six). Obviously, again, to both the Jew and Christian the basic human experience concerns a specific theme: *Nature and Grace* (Chapter Seven).

Chapter Eight considers man within an *Evolutionary Perspective*, or as he confronts a dynamic, yet unified, whole grounded in a mysterious freedom.

Finally, man is a being who hopes; so in the *Ninth and concluding Chapter* we confront man's *Hope in Eternal Life*.

The *Conclusion* summarizes the results of such an enquiry.

What I write in this book comes completely from my personal understanding at this moment of my life. My indebtedness to others will be apparent from the quotations, footnote references, and the bibliography. What I have learned from others, including the designated teaching authorities in the church, has come to cohere in my mind as a living unity. I am particularly grateful to all those whose kindness, influence, and help supported me as I was engaged in writing the book. In this regard I owe much thanks to the Nursing Sisters of the Sick Poor, Jamaica, L. I. My thanks are due to Sr. M. Salome, OSB, San Diego, Cal., who both edited and typed the original manuscript. I am also grateful to Gabriel Cusimano, CP, who proofread the galley pages. I am most grateful to Mrs. Jean Breig who both read and edited the book at each and every stage; and to Mr. John Breig who designed the book.

Contents

the
MYSTERY
of
MAN

Introduction

1. *Man* is a living embodied unit open to the infinite. The center of so defining man is found within our person. We speak of this as man's self-understanding confronting the universe. We know we possess a body. We know we are alive. We know we possess a mysterious life principle. We perceive our intuitions or insights into the meaning of reality. We observe our transcendental tendencies as we search for life, unity, truth, beauty, goodness and love. We know that we are an open being on our way to some final destiny. In such a context we say that man is an incarnate spirit. Yet what man really is and the ultimate meaning of human existence are hidden in our particular future and the event of death. We are always living, thinking, speaking, acting in this world and on this side of death. At some point each man confronts himself as a mystery. At every moment man is a problem to himself.

Man questions himself constantly about the essence of his nature, the meaning of his life, the end results. He objectifies perceived meaning in words and definitions; he socializes it in building community with his fellow men. He thinks and acts guided by the principle: phenomena disclose the intelligibility of reality. He will look at everything related to himself: his person, knowledge, experience, love, freedom, meaning, the world, community. He will say what these point to and order his life in a specific direction. Human existence, itself, verifies or questions the evidence pictured out in statements of human judgment.

Actually, one can define man in two possible ways. He can speak of man in terms related to *objective* evidence. An emphasis is given to ideas associated with empirical fact. On the other hand, one can speak of man in terms related to the *perceived meaning* associated with the world of phenomena. In this approach an emphasis is given to ideas associated with human insight.

Following the first method, one may define man as a noble savage whose goodness must be protected constantly from corruption. Or, again, one may say that man is an ignoble savage whose destructive tendencies must constantly be fought and subdued.

1

Again, following B. F. Skinner, one may take a neutral experimental view of man. He can say that man is basically a responding animal, reacting to stimuli associated with rewards and punishments. One manipulates man through environmental conditions.

Such definitions cause little or no trouble to modern man. He can live and work with each or all of them. They may help him to survive in a particular environment. But one cannot use them to perceive the intelligibility in his personal life and ultimate destiny. At some point, scientific empirical definitions of man solve nothing while raising questions pertaining to meaning.

Western rational tradition followed the second possibility and defined man more from a method of human insight or self-understanding. Heraclitus had perceived that you will not find the limits of the soul, though you take every road. Sophocles understood the creative openness found in man. He has resources for almost everything. From baffling maladies he devises escape. Only against death shall he call for aid in vain. Socrates was certain that no evil could conquer a good man in life or death. For Plato, man's self-knowledge pertained to the very essence of knowledge. Aristotle perceived that a soul is the cause, ground, or life-principle of the human body. Augustine wrote in his *Confessions*: "I directed my thoughts to myself and said, 'Who are you?' And I answered, 'A man.' And lo, in me there appear both body and soul, the one without, the other within" (*Confessions*, bk. 10, ch. 6). When Thomas Aquinas looked at man, he saw him as he existed in the real world yet his basic judgments rested on insight. As he looked at man's acts, perceived from within, he affirmed that the life principle in man transcended matter. Why? Because man knew things like stones in a manner that transcended particular stones. Man knew stones intellectually. "There exists, therefore, an operation of the soul which so far exceeds the corporeal nature that it is not even performed by any corporeal organ; and such is the operation of the rational soul" (*Summa Theologiae*, I, ques. 78, art. 1). Nicholas of Cusa in his work on *Learned Ignorance* turned the definition of man away from his proper acts towards man's remembrance of what he is. In such a recall man perceives that

2

human nature contains in itself intellectual and sensible natures and, therefore, embraces within itself all things. Man is the microcosm or the universe in miniature.

Following this second direction of man's self-understanding of himself, one may define man as an incarnate knowing subject (or self) open to the infinite. One is saying that man is a specific something: an essence, yet an open essence (facing new and old possibilities). Man is a mysterious personal act of existing with transcendental tendencies.

Some will say that the statements about man passed down through tradition are self-evident or obvious. Yet, at every period men recognize that all their affirmations about man point to a profound mystery. We perceive, as did Nicholas of Cusa, that the secret of the universe is disclosed in man. One no longer faces an anthropological question but the essence of reality itself. In this perspective the problems of ontology are not thrown off to some world beyond our physical world of space and time but directed towards the inner depths of each man.

2. *Anthropology*, in general, is the study of both the nature and mystery of man. It attempts to objectify in greater detail one of the two ways by which we define man. Following the first method of observing empirical evidence, it will construct an ordered phenomenology of man. Such a method, as we have suggested, ends in raising new questions and leads, by man's inner need to know the whole truth, to an intuitional anthropology. This is an anthropology of the spirit. It seeks to perceive and say something true and of value in answer to two basic questions: What is man? What is the meaning of human existence? It indicates particular data, analyzes the data through human insight and reflection, and affirms through judgments some viewpoint about man and human existence.

Theological anthropology is the study of man from the perspective of God as a personal creator and savior. It affirms—from what man perceives, experiences, is conscious of—that man's origin, nature, and continued existence are from this immanent yet transcendent Absolute or Ground. It declares that the meaning and

3

destiny of man are to be found in a life of dialogue and communion with God and his fellow men. What is experienced as making sense as man confronts himself, this world, *the whole*, in a communal solidarity with other human persons, is the affirmation: God is the *life* of man. One cannot prove such a statement; rather such a judgment is the objectification of a fundamental experience related to a man's total action. In and through a confrontation with an immanent holy Mystery a person finds himself; seeks, finds, and serves others; seeks, finds, and serves society. Somewhat as the sun gives light to the darkness of the dawn, a personal Absolute is experienced as the *Light* to the darkness of the human condition. As the world fades away or leaves man empty after giving him all its gifts, men confess, or hope, that God is the *goal* or destiny of all their actions.

Theological anthropology begins its study and explanation of the mystery of man from a center found in man himself: man's self-consciousness and personal experience. It does not say that man perceives the Presence of God directly but through the mediation of what a man experiences himself to be.

When we really understand a poem, all we know of the poet is what we learn of him in the poem—no biographical wisdom is of value for the pure understanding of what is to be understood: the *I* which approaches us is the subject of this single poem. But when we read other poems by the poet in the same true way, their subjects combine in all their multiplicity, completing and confirming one another, to form the one polyphony of the person's existence.
In such a way, out of the givers of the signs, the speakers of the words of lived life, out of the moment Gods there arises for us with a single identity the Lord of the voice, the One.[1]

The basic *principle for interpretation*—the hermeneutic principle —is human self-understanding, yet as an acting self in a living personal relationship with the whole of reality. An emphasis is always placed on the *present moment*, or on the way present human experience receives genuine meaning. The task is to develop such a self-understanding into a Christian viewpoint through clear ideas, affirmations, and indicated distinctions and relationships.

---

[1] Martin Buber, *Between Man and Man*, London, 1947, p. 15.

The Word of God as revelation is the self-manifestation of the creating and loving Presence of God in the whole of reality: the divine *Logos* (or the Intelligible Principle, immanent in all things) creation, history, persons, especially Jesus Christ as the risen Lord. In some real sense the whole of reality is a revealing word. God speaks to each of us through the mediation of everything. The active principle of our knowing and understanding such a revelation is twofold: God's dynamic disclosing Presence (the Spirit) and man's total self and action.

I call such a perspective an *existential-ontological* religious viewpoint, for it serves as the basis of our decisions and action without pretending to have all the answers or the whole truth, and one senses at the same time that he knows and understands the depths of reality within himself though darkly and in a relative manner. We confront the depths of our inner experience while living in the dimensions of meaning as if a light were shining in the darkness.

An *historical* factor must also be indicated. Often truth, as personally experienced, cannot be objectified with simple clear ideas and affirmations. Our subjective life is a constant questing openness. Our present dimensions of meaning can be clarified somewhat through past historical events or records. In this context past traditions with all their objectified representations and affirmations—thus the Bible—clarify or question present human experience.

Rational and categorical answers, however, often hide false certainties. Who among us can wipe away the darkness associated with every moment of human existence? Who among us can wipe away the darkness associated with human death? Difficulties, then, regarding answering questions about man in terms of reason and set categories suggest that no one can write a theological anthropology like a solution to a puzzle. Rather, meaning presses upon our life. It invades everything we do. It dawns upon us out of the night. At times the only way we can conquer our doubts and misgivings is in creating meaning in our own personal life. We work out the meaning of things. We must add, further, that the deepest and most sensible answers are given through shared human love. "Let us love one another, for love is of God, and he who loves is born of God and knows God. He who does not love does not know God; for God is love" (1 Jn. 4. 7-8).

As a man takes the inward journey towards the depths of his experience how does he account for the fundamental meaning which human existence seems to possess? Or we ask the same question another way: What may be said about man's ability to know, even as we realize the limitations and deficiencies of our rational ideas or projected pictures of reality? Or, again, we ask: Just what is the horizon, the circle, or the end point of man's knowledge? The principle guiding theological anthropology is the affirmation that the inward horizon of man's total experience extends to *the whole of reality*. Man has true insights, or intuitions, into the intelligibility of the whole as both unified in himself yet diverse. Matter is not spirit. Man is not the ultimate Ground of his essence or existence. This is not to say or assume that man knows everything about reality. All he knows begins and ends in darkness. He need only close his eyes and look within himself to realize this. Man's viewpoint is always limited and differs from man to man. Yet, in turning inward, man confronts the whole and experiences its depths.

Man's journey inward is towards spirit and the source of all that is. But what is the nature of this Ground? It cannot be seen, grasped, captured, bargained with. It is undefinable, indescribable, mysterious, good, holy. Is it personal or impersonal? The Eastern world answers vaguely: "The Self is the lord of all; inhabitant of the hearts of all. He is the source of all; creator and dissolver of beings." The Judaic-Christian religion proclaims, or confesses what it experiences, that the ultimate Ground within man is an immanent yet transcendent personal Presence. In Him we live, move, and have our being.

Both the religious man in the East and West takes the journey inward. Each prays: "Lead me from the unreal to the real. Lead me from darkness to light. Lead me from death to immortality." Each lives by faith and hope. Each knows that the only real proof of God's existence is a living union with Him.

6

One may reply, and many do today, that man's self-understanding of himself as a conscious subject leads him to affirm that man is no more than a transcendent form of *matter*. Such a response is not necessarily fallacious. Obviously man is a unity of incarnate existence. But, in such a context, the basic question is placed: Does man's inward journey end in no more than an ocean of material energy? This is both an open and honest question. Each man through a lifetime asks himself the question many times and in many different ways. The question expresses genuine human doubts and fears as each person faces the confusion and darkness of his own life. The question is never completely removed. Faith is a light shining in darkness. How can we expect, demand, or find some incontrovertible, once-for-all proof?

What Theological Anthropology is able to say, and does say, is: The meaning of the universe, or the whole of reality, is disclosed in what lies before us; and this intelligibility is centered in man and his daily life.

3. Man's living union with God is spoken of at times as a *life of grace*. God's grace, or favor, is *his* free and loving turning to each and every human person. It is God's immanent, creating, and loving Presence. Yet it is a life in dialogue. In some real sense God waits upon man and answers him. A free personal encounter is implied. "There is no distinction between Jew and Greek; the same Lord is Lord of all and bestows his riches upon all who call upon him. For everyone who calls upon the name of the Lord will be saved" (Rom. 10. 12-3).

On God's side, grace is God himself, a personal dynamic Act of existing. Grace is God's creating and loving Presence in and among men.

On man's part, grace is a *life* which a human person shares with God. Because grace pertains to a man's personal life and experience, it possesses a dimension of human consciousness. Who and what man is, then, has a created meaning in his daily conscious life, especially the consciousness of free love offered and shared.

The *Christian community* is a visible manifestation, sign, or sacrament of God's loving Presence working through the dynamic power (the Spirit) of the risen Jesus. The dead and risen Jesus is experienced and confessed to be the divine Lord.

Yet the Christian community is only a sign or sacrament of what God is doing in and among all men in a less visible way. The Logos, or the divine Word, manifests his dynamic Presence in the whole of creation and in all that happens. The life of every man is a receiving and a call. The events that happen to him are the signs of his being addressed.

4. One last remark seems necessary. A man's intuitive perception or intuition into the meaning of reality need not be faith and should be distinguished from faith. Faith, in its strict sense, is man's living and free response to God's Presence and address. A human intuition or experience is implied, but the central element is the response. Faith is an answer to a call. "Speak, Lord, for your servant hears" (1 Sam. 3.9).

Again, the object of faith is not reality, or man, or history, but man's living encounter with God. It is always an ending—a shared communion and dialogue with God—and a new beginning with unknown possibilities.

Chapter 1

The Problematic of Man

General Observations

Anthropology is the human study of both the nature and mystery of man. It is man's reflection upon himself as he seeks to penetrate into the meaning or sense of his essence, his life, and his destiny. One examines all the data associated with the human body and inner human experience, indicates the evidence, and offers one or more possible explanations. The data, itself, is extremely extensive, covering the whole of the empirical sciences. All of this is centered in some way on man and his life. The whole seeks to shed some light on the nature of man and the facts associated with human life.

All the data associated with man and his life, however, are given and examined in a form of questioning. Man is a problem to himself. There is some aspect hidden in the body, the flesh, the tissues, the cells of man that is mysterious and always escaping the deepest scrutiny. Every insight and statement about man at some point leads to apparent contradictions or a tension of opposite elements. A biologist, when speaking about living cells and organs in man, utters the word "chance" and immediately adds the term "necessity."[1] One is unable to unravel the puzzle.

If one says that man is a material object, the existence of man's person or ego seems to contradict such a position. Yet to say, on the other hand, that man is a personal, self-conscious subject seems to contradict the obvious fact that man is a material embodied thing. The most apparent fact to every man is his body. One can, of course, say that his self-consciousness is an illusion; yet some form of self-consciousness is a phenomenon experienced by a

---

[1] cf., J. Monod, *Le Hasard et la Nécessité*, Paris, 1970.

man's journey inward to the depths of his body.

Each man lives in and through a particular organization of material energy and experiences the meaning of human existence in and through material energy. But such a statement leads to controversy, for at the same time man experiences a transcending personal knowledge, freedom, decision, responsibility. He is aware that he possesses a life principle. He then speaks of spirit or soul as the primary principle of inner subjectivity.

But even here one is not able to fix or define his exact view. At one moment he is speaking of his body; and then, suddenly, he is speaking of himself. At one moment he is saying "Yes" to one aspect of himself; and then, suddenly, he is saying "No." At one moment he is saying that one can speak of man only in terms of scientific evidence; and then, suddenly, he speaks in terms of inner personal intuition with a strong sense of certainty. The paradoxes of what and how a man knows himself becomes evident in his language, judgments, and reasons. All his self discoveries and statements seem so terminal; but often, when he watches a person die, he is reduced to a shocked silence. Just what is the exact and fixed picture of man?

Again, a man must make fundamental commitments in and through his body. He must depend on the energy within himself whether he is young or old, on an amount of oxygen, on food and heat, on the strength of his physical senses at set times and places. Then, suddenly, he risks everything on an experience of truth, freedom, love, justice. At one moment a man's life answers are proclaiming that all is flesh; and then, to the contrary, he indicates by his actions that man must live on a spiritual energy, personal commitment, and responsible free reactions to the persons he meets in his world. At one moment man complains about old age and death; then, suddenly, he smiles and celebrates the joy and fulfillment of present values. At one moment man's total action suggests that the secret of everything is found in dirt and mud; then, suddenly, he lives out of the strange experience of intellectual act. Human beings live and suffer and die within the tensions of such paradoxes and contradictions.

10

In the midst of such questioning where do we center the problem? The answer to this question appears to be: in man himself. If man is the microcosm, or the sign of the meaning of the universe in miniature, then the fundamental problem of any anthropology is rooted in man himself and his self-understanding. And such a self-understanding is related to the whole of reality. Just why and how does man sense that the whole has meaning?

The problem of man and meaning are associated with every moment of a man's existence. Our answers are never complete; and in all his answers a man is ever questioning and wondering. In real concrete human life not only is man a thing that understands objective reality and understands himself, but at the same time man is the thing that understands reality and himself in and through an inner personal experience associated with a particular time and place. In this context not only does man raise objective and essential questions asking: What is man? What is the meaning or sense of human existence? But he asks the same questions continually in a personal, existential way: Who am I? What is the meaning of my existence? We are able to observe these two manners of questioning when we study the history of religions and the history of philosophical anthropology.

The Problem of Human Essence

1. While man is and remains a problem and mystery to himself, basic facts appear obvious as minimal foundations for further disclosure: first, man is an organized material object; and second, man possesses a life principle that is unified in some way through his body. The first fact is obvious through empirical evidence. Man can see and sense the presence of his body. The second fact is obvious from the standpoint of immediate, lived, inner, intuitive experience. A man will say: I am alive. What he experiences within himself is confirmed by external observation. Man senses the difference between a stone and a living organism. He observes some difference between an alive and a dead tree, an alive and dead dog, an alive and dead man. He will ask another man at

11

the time of an accident: Are you alive? Are you conscious? Are you all there?

From these two points of departure man explains himself further by added experience. In such an extended context man experiences himself to be a living embodied unit, a personal self, free, conscious of self-consciousness, open to understanding, open to factors of reality that seem to transcend material energy. Yet, at some juncture this problem arises: What is man? Just what does one mean when he says that man is a unified coincidence of opposites—*coincidentia oppositorum*—matter and spirit.

To say that man is an embodied living self seems both true and obvious. In some real way it appears to be true and obvious to say that man possesses a life principle; but to say that man is an embodied *spirit* creates all manner of problems. What is one saying, what does one mean when he says that the life principle of man is *spirit?* Hegel, of course, would say that spirit is self-conscious mind, adding two other observations: first, the being of mind is its *act*, and its act is to be aware of itself; second, the unity of mind, or spirit, in man comes to have its oneness in and through an otherness: Matter. What Hegel indicates appears to be true from the standpoint of man's consciousness. Man is a self-existent self-consciousness. But such observations are not obvious from the standpoint of empirical science. What one sees and senses is only matter. One cannot see spirit; nor can one feel or sense spirit. Man's life principle or spirit is always self-referring; that is, it always refers a human person back to his own ego and to his consciousness and self-understanding. The suspicion is present, at times, that we may be losing ourself in an illusion of self-consciousness.

Again, we must notice the crux of the problem. To speak of *spirit* one must refer ultimately to his own personal self-consciousness and his living realtionship with other human persons. What is *spirit* in man is his self-conscious act of existing. In such a context of meaning, that man is spirit seems obvious, or appears to be obvious, to his self-conscious awareness; but once man's attention moves from his inner center of self-awareness towards an otherness found in his body—matter—the nature of what one means by the term *spirit* becomes ever more problematic. What, exactly, does one mean when he uses the word *spirit* in referring back to his ego's self-consciousness and understanding?

Often, in our modern world, we end up the dialogue by not referring to *truth* as such, but to a person's self-experience. We say: You must *find* and *discover* yourself. What such a position implies is the insight that the *essence* of man is his manner of possessing or having existence and is to be known and understood in the context of one's own life. The Western classical viewpoint says, essence (*essentia*) follows or flows out of the act of existing (*esse*).

But to say that the essence of what man is follows upon his act of existing and is known and understood in the context of self-knowledge and self-understanding suggests an endless search and openness in a person's wandering through this world. This is not to infer that one cannot or does not know himself and reality. Actually man is the thing in this world who can know and understand himself and reality. Such a statement only indicates the phenomenon of what a man is. Yet, at the same time man knows himself and reality only in the context of his own life associated with a particular time and place. In such a condition he continually places the question: What is it *all* about?

An added factor touching on man's self-understanding of himself is his *eyes*. Modern man seeks or tends to verify everything in and through his senses, especially the eyes. Today man says: The eyes have it. What modern man cannot see or verify through his senses, especially his eyes (empirical evidence), he will not believe.

The human eyes sense like a camera. They engage in a material or physical seeing. They capture only a material picture of what man is, an image, a symbol.

As a man looks at himself and other men, he materializes the essence of man. He sees no more than a material thing, though in the context of his own life. The more he looks at his own face changing to an oldness and a dying, the more he becomes uncertain, anxious, confused. He repeats over and over: Just who and what am I? The more a man looks at himself with his eyes, the more he distrusts deeper forms of human knowing. The more a man looks at himself with his eyes the more he senses the picture: an organized complex of material energy. In such a context, what meaning have the words "I," "You," "We?"

Sociology and *psychology* can and will say, of course, that man lives within a field of tensions, a tension of living relationships with himself and others. Yet such empirical answers only raise the question: What is the center of such personal relations? Man's inner journey confronts again a self-understanding presence. One encounters himself and other human persons only through such a personal mystery.

2. Men throughout the course of history have faced the problematic of man. They have, in general, recognized the two basic facts about the mystery of the human self: the material body and a unified life principle. Any answers given have been the explanation and representation of reflective discernment associated with a continuous human experience. Experience discloses the tissue of sense or meaning. Yet the answers have differed and, as a consequence, been called in question.

The first and most radical explanation has been the viewpoint: man possesses *no specific essence* or nature. Man has no closed and fixed manner of existing. What each man possesses is a stream of embodied existence.

Such an answer emphasizes the change and historicity of man. He is a dynamic and changing thing, living in a material world of time and space. According to such a view, no one can say with any certainty what man is or what he will become. Changes in his body effect changes within man's very self. Man constantly changes himself, creates himself, destroys himself.

This is the viewpoint of Jean Paul Sartre and his followers. The terms I, You, We, point to no particular essence. Man is an historical thing open and subject to constant change. Man is what one thinks himself to be or what he wills himself to be in this world, having received with his origin a thrust into existence and towards existence. "Man is nothing else but what he makes of himself."[2]

---

[2] Jean Paul Sartre, *Existentialism and Human Emotions*, New York, 1957, p. 15.

A second explanation affirms that man does possess a specific nature or essence; but it is *an open essence*. We may define man in a general way as a rational animal. Yet what man is and what he may become cannot be defined within the framework of such an exact image or picture. This strange openness found in every man is centered in his life principle, the soul of a man. No one can say with a certain exactness what man may become.

Such an explanation was suggested by Aristotle when he wrote in his *De Anima* that the soul of man is in a certain sense everything. Every human, concrete condition particularizes a person, but no one is able to imagine what man can become and yet remain a man.

Any stress on man's openness to new possibilities turns this viewpoint towards the first answer.

A third answer affirms that man is not only a *particular essence* but possesses unique characteristics through which one is and remains a man. These characteristics are: embodiment and self-perceiving subject. Man is an embodied spirit. According to this view, man to be man must always have some living relationship to matter.

This perspective is, perhaps, the most widely accepted explanation of man's essence. Man is a unity of matter and spirit and is the representative form of such a unity.[3] The spirit of man in such a context is the unifying living power or principle in the matter. Such a perspective also implies that if man survives death he does so in some living relationship to matter. One can transcend what he is on this side of the grave provided he remains embodied spirit.

A fourth answer stresses the *existential* characteristics associated with man. The emphasis is on the personal rather than on a nature. It is said that a man exists with a *Dasein*, a particular *thereness* with a set space and time. One both manifests himself and is absorbed into a situation and the constant present moment. Man exists every moment in a particular time and place with a particular open freedom. Man becomes authentically human only when he lives freely and is able to find himself in every present moment.

This viewpoint stresses a person's immediate personal knowledge,

[3] C. Hörgl and F. Rauh (ed.) *Grenzfragen des Glaubens, Einsiedeln,* 1967, pg. 46-7.

15

knowledge of the immediate, or what *is*. One starts and proceeds in an immediate way accepting what is given. It becomes suspicious of imaged representations (what one pictures man to be) and of any closed system of ideas about man.

Our understanding of man in general and of any concrete man in particular is very much confused by the fact that the composition of man is complex and it is not an easy matter to reduce the complexity to a unity. Personality in man is the result of conflict. It is the multiple composition of man that made possible those ancient conceptions which admitted the existence of a shadow, of a double of man; and it was difficult to decide which was the principal reality. There is no doubt ego in man—the true, the real, the deep ego, and the ego which is created by the imagination and the passions, which is fictitious and which drags man downwards. Personality is worked out by a long drawn out process, by choice, by the crowding out of that which is in me but is not my ego.[4]

Personal, immediate knowledge of what is appears to be the richest human knowledge. Its treasures of insight cover every moment of a lifetime and are given in the situation of every concrete moment and place. Yet a paradox is also present. Such a viewpoint states what a person knows and experiences. "This is how it is with me." It is a position of personal self-understanding, but it gives no content of truth about the exact *nature* of man. One possesses a real and deep consciousness of *how it is* with him, but the problematic of what man is (his essence) remains.

This fourth answer is the viewpoint of Kierkegaard, K. Jaspers, and Martin Heidegger. One experiences the essence of human existence, but one does not know the exact essence of man. The answer to the problematic of man is given in the future with the moment of death.

The Problem of Meaning

1. Every human person in some real manner follows the fourth viewpoint. This is to say that for the most part man begins or starts with his immediate knowledge, his immediate experience of what is. Such a perception, however, is very shallow; and since man is a questioning being, at his better moments he seeks to live

---

[4] N. Berdyaev, *The Divine and the Human*, London, 1949, p. 112.

within the horizon of intelligibility or of what makes sense. This is to question the whatness, or the essence, of things.

If we say what man is—an embodied spirit—we must be able to describe the characteristics of man through distinct combinations of words and sentences and find some principle which controls our affirmations. This principle would appear to be: man is the being who intuits and understands the intelligibility of reality. Such insights of meaning are expressed out of the mind of the human self as its truth. The intelligibility of reality is given in the real world, in what lies before one. The meaning of things is found in their actual existence. Such reality exists and stands as it is even though it is not known fully.

The intelligibility of reality, however, is mediated through the human mind. In this context we say: man is the being in whom the meaning of being is disclosed. He is the one who through self-understanding and reflective awareness raises and answers the questions of intelligibility.

If we are able to say that it is proper to man to perceive and understand the meaning or intelligibility which reigns in everything that is, such an affirmation must be qualified.

First, Heidegger speaks of man's *forgetfulness* of being. Man is an embodied being who lives in this world of space and time. Often he is more practical than intuitive. He perceives little meaning in questioning the intelligibility of things in this world with the purpose of reflecting on it, to ponder what might be its truth. Rather, he seeks to deal with things as sense-certainty discloses their nature. This situation also suggests that man's experienced meaning rises out of a world of total human action rather than out of some narrow world of a perceiving *I*. Again, man's experience of meaning is related to and constituted by his relations to other persons. Man experiences meaning as he lives in close community relations with his fellow men. Problems and questions arise every moment and from every side.

Second, man's knowledge of reality is finite and tends towards constant inquiry. Man lives in this world and experiences reality through a light that ends in an ocean of darkness. Man's knowledge

17

is always light in darkness. The visible world itself appears as a world of paradoxes, a coincidence of opposites.

At the same time we notice that man's knowledge of the intelligibility of reality is not pure thought but associated with the total action of what he is: a manner of *living experience*. I know about reality in and through my finite experience. At the same time we must add the insight that man can and does know reality in and through his *ideas*. Further, man states what he experiences and knows through spiritual forms of judgments; and these human judgments, in turn, express the thematic content found in a person's experience of what is. Finally, a man's perception of the intelligibility of reality is always mediated through some specific form of consciousness.

2. Sartre says, of course, that the world-for-man comes to have meaning in and through the acts of man's consciousness. Any thing that can bring about a harmony between man and the objects of this world is obviously disclosed to a man in and through a human self-awareness. Men experience meaning living in this world. They do so within their own inner solitude and with a sense of personal responsibility. But, Sartre would add, the whole of reality has no meaning. An immanent-transcendent personal God does not exist. Man is a traveler on a journey to nothingness. We live in this world looking at each other, feeling uncomfortable, until our train comes to the last stop where no one is waiting. Man is condemned by chance to live in an absurd situation. He experiences meaning. He is conscious of his own freedom and feels a real sense of personal responsibility. But the whole of reality has no meaning; or, if it has, man cannot figure it out.

I'm answerable only to them who are answerable only to God, and I don't believe in God. So try to figure it out. As for me, I can't, and I sometimes wonder whether I'm not playing winner loses and not trying hard to stamp out my one-time hopes so that everything will be restored to me a hundred-fold.[5]

Sartre raises an unique problematic associated with a man's existence in this world. We can say, and must say, that we experience

---

[5] Jean-Paul Sartre, *The Words*, New York, 1964, p. 254.

meaning living in our world. We experience this meaning in a context of real personal freedom and responsibility. Yet the whole of reality *may* not have meaning. We may meet no one when we get off the train. My consciousness is there and cannot be thought away; but, perhaps, I have an idealism of meaning which is illusory. Is there any sense, or intelligibility, to the whole of reality?

Obviously modern man is much like Sartre. He wonders if anyone will be present when he gets off the train. Yet, at the same time we observe that man in his consciousness wonders about the meaning of the whole of reality and about his final destiny. We are able to say that man in his self-awareness has a concern and direction towards the whole of reality and its possible transcendent sense.

In some real way man experiences himself to be a being ordered towards the meaning of the whole, ordered towards the transcendent, ordered towards an Absolute that must be both transcendent to man yet immanent in him. In this context, men would say in past ages that man is a being ordered towards God. One may, of course, wonder or affirm that this Absolute does not exist. He may refuse to be open to the problem and the call of God. But by doing so, he renders his existence absurd. His life in such a horizon is good for nothing.

Man certainly is a being open to the whole of reality. Man certainly is a being concerned about the meaning of the whole of reality. Man certainly is a being concerned about his ultimate destiny. At some point, the question about man becomes a problem about God's existence. The problem is this: is *being* to be identified with this world, or is there a transcendent yet immanent Ground?

3. Again, when we consider the problematic of man and meaning, we must notice the importance of a *psychological factor*: man experiences meaning in his life in a human condition of *shared love*, in a restfulness we call *peace*. A perception of meaning is often lost when his personal, social, and historical conditions change.

Human life appears to have meaning when one is young and in love. Life takes on new depths of meaning when one has his own family, children, friends, position, social and historical justice and peace. Life seems to lose meaning when one grows old and fails to experience shared love; when he loses his family, children, friends, position; when he no longer shares in a common justice and peace.

No reason for living can supplant man's need for shared affection. Man needs love to affirm meaning. This does not disqualify intelligibility but suggests its relative importance in the psychological experience of a human person. The human self is not an isolated individual. The self is a *person* and personal existence is constituted by shared affection among persons. In the same context God is experienced as a personal, loving Ground. When one is unloved, the world appears to be an obstacle; one experiences a lossness; he cannot consent to his own person. It is said, as a consequence, that a man finds himself in and through the *love* of other persons.

From a *biological* point of view we speak of man as a living organized unit ordered towards death. Death is the end of man as we know him through our eyes. Yet man is more than this. As a person man is the being-together with other persons in love. He cannot be a person in life, or death, without love.

In the context of shared personal love, human death may not necessarily destroy the meaning of human existence. Death could be the decisive moment of man's being in this world and the door leading into the hall of ultimate and eternal meaning.

The Problem of Human Death

It is good news for every man to hear and understand that he is a being who truly perceives the meaning inherent in the things of this world. It is good news, further, to hear and understand that man is a being truly open to the whole of reality, to the infinite, to the transcendent. Man perceives the meaning found in his world. He is free. He possesses real responsibility. But all this is associated with his life in this world.

What takes place when he dies? Obviously man is a being ordered towards this end. We need only observe the possible events associated with the life of other human persons. But, death is an event which happens to other people. It has not happened, as yet, to a human person living in this world. We can only say, from the evidence of appearance that death is the end of man as we know him.

The exact *meaning*, then, of the human event of death cannot be perceived by anyone who raises the question of its meaning. Why is this? Because he can only raise the problem of death on this side of the end. Man's experience of meaning is disclosed to him in his world of space and time. Meaning is always given to each man in the present moment and within this world. The experiences of the meaning of death belongs to a future which carries man beyond space and time.

We tend today, as I have said, to define man as embodied spirit. We add to this the observation that man's living experience of transcendence is associated with his *spirit*. We recall the insight of Thomas Aquinas that the act of intelligence transcends time (*Intellectus est supra tempus*). But such affirmations do not offer an answer to the problem of death, though they might point to one. One realizes this the nearer he approaches death.

Some might think that "death" is the problem and "immortality" is the answer. But is this not too simple? St. Augustine, for example, asks: "Do you really know yourself to be immortal?" He replies: "I do not know. But suppose you experienced yourself to be immortal? Would that be enough? It would be indeed a great thing, but to me it would still be something very slight."[6]

Yet, at times, to say that something discloses slight meaning is to affirm something that should be said. But what is man saying of his spirit when he speaks of death? He is referring to the intelligibility found in himself and reality. Augustine would say: "I perceive an exact and all embracing order."[7] In my spirit, through my self-awareness, I perceive an intelligibility which seems to transcend space and time.

Yet the problem of the meaning of death remains. Rational inductions and deductions are never satisfactory. They extend beyond

[6] St. Augustine, *Soliloquy* 2. 1
[7] Ibid., 2, 2: "*Manifestissimum ordinem video atque brevissimum.*"

the living experience of the human person. Both the problematic of what man is and what he will become must be experienced. Meaning, or lack of meaning, is given in and through the living experience. One must experience every "Yes" and "No" embodied in his nature, the light and darkness of intelligibility, the mystery of death. In this framework, the answer to the problem of death—if there is an answer—is given in death.

In *religious experience* men perceive and bear witness to a Holy Presence. "The Lord God helps me; therefore I have not been confounded . . . He who vindicates me is near" (Is. 50. 7-8). From this standpoint one trusts God in death. He is the Lord of both the living and the dead. In life, the answers God gives are given in and through a living shared experience. One hopes through this Presence that the call of God is to eternal life.

The Problem of Christian Anthropology

Christian anthropology begins with the religious perception—or faith response—that the intelligibility of reality is disclosed in man, in his personal life, in his personal relationships with God and his fellow men. This experience is a community awareness and takes place in an historical and social context. The meaning experienced is a form of living awareness associated with human consciousness. The meaning experienced is one of life, love, freedom, peace, hope.

The Gospel—or good news—of Christianity is the affirmation that God offers to every man a new life in and through the dynamic Presence of the dead and risen Jesus.

Such a faith experience is expressed by Paul, the apostle, in the earliest New Testament witness: ". . . you turned to God from idols, to serve a living and true God, and to wait for his Son from heaven, whom he raised from the dead, Jesus who delivers us from the wrath to come" (1 Th. 1. 9-10). The thinking is imagined within the framework of an ancient cosmology. The dead and risen Jesus lives in God. God dwells in heaven, far above the world. We can say that the cosmic picture expresses both the transcendent and immanent Presence of God in and through the risen Lord.

22

But here the problem arises. What are the intelligible aspects of such a proclamation placed as it is within a cosmic horizon?

Christian anthropology centers the answer in man. But this answer must have some reference to time and place, to the Presence of God and Christ in our world, to creation, to the mystery of sin in man's world, to nature and grace, the Church, and the fulfillment of man's destiny in death.

Today we look at man from our present knowledge and our total living experience. Our present human understanding of man helps us to correct or explain man's past mythological understanding. At the same time, the past Christian viewpoint proclaims to our present experience that the foundation of man, the meaning of his life, and his destiny, lies in God and his loving Presence.

Christian anthropology is a viewpoint about man's nature and destiny based on religious experience, yet associated with the total human experience. It is a viewpoint of an *historical* community which seeks to integrate the present with the past, and the past with the present.

Still, at the same time, man is a mystery. The problematic of man remains. The Christian, at least by intention, is open to both the problem and call of God. This means that he must remain open to the problematic of man.

Chapter 2

Philosophical Anthropology

General Observations

Having considered the problematic associated with the mystery of man's nature and destiny, we understand that one can still affirm: Man is the being in whom the meaning of reality is disclosed though in a context of place and time.

Man perceives meaning, or intelligibility, or the sense of reality, in and through his total human action. Meaning comes to one's self-understanding, however, through our *intellectual* consciousness and self-reflection.

To be a man, one is thrown into a situation of perceiving meaning, searching for meaning, creating meaning. This is man's journey, inward and outward, through the body, undertaken in the context of each present moment. Man senses that he undertakes this task freely and of his own personal responsibility. Each man undertakes this action on his own. He may perceive meaning in many different ways. He may perceive meaning from various possible standpoints. When, however, he seeks to unify his knowledge in terms of man's basic nature, he undertakes a task called *Philosophical Anthropology*.

In general, we define *philosophical anthropology* as the study of man's being. It seeks to answer the questions: Who or what is man? What is the meaning of man's existence? It has for its object the total whole of human life. It can be distinguished from a particular empirical science, which studies man from a limited viewpoint, either as a physical organized object, a living organized being, or a thinking subject. In this way philosophical anthropology seeks to establish intimacy with the human condition and go beyond

24

the world of physiology, biology, and psychology.

One, however, may question the possibility of making any statement about man from such an overall or integral viewpoint. The light we have about man is in the context of space and time. How can we know the total order or the final system of things? When we examine our life it appears as an adventure. We begin it over from moment to moment. Harmonious systemizations seem to belong to the past.

The problem, however, indicates the originality of philosophical anthropology. It treats the subject of man not in the context of some system, but in reference to reality. Man, to be himself, cannot go on from moment to moment merely enjoying life. At some moment, some place, he must take a stand about the meaning of the whole. In such a situation he may, and should, use all the evidence at his command. His final and deepest inference must be one of intellectual insight. Such an effort is one of necessity if he is to face the real world and survive as a human being. Without such insights one lives a worthless and stunted life without an horizon.

Man's intellectual search for meaning, however, is always associated with a dialectic of unified opposites or contraries: being and nothingness, unity and complexity, the whole and the part, actuality and potency, essence and existence, matter and form, intelligence and energy, body and life principle, matter and spirit, intelligence and will, reality and its foundation. One factor or element is not the other in an exact sense; yet the one is united to the other in a living relationship. Man in himself and in relationship to other men is, as Hegel has said, a realization of a community of conscious life. In man the opposites or contraries of matter and spirit come to a transcending unity of self-consciousness. In this experience there is a movement along the highway of truth towards the real, towards the whole, towards the infinite, towards the eternal, towards the Holy. One experiences meaning in the context of a unified whole; yet man's insights do not reveal the final Ground of the inner reality.

Perhaps the Ground is a nothingness or mere matter. Man, it is perceived, moves along the highway of truth. But what is at the end of the last avenue? The light of human consciousness comes to a darkness. An absolute lucidity makes one smile.

Facing the *opposites* in man and searching for a unity of significance, philosophical anthropology makes two kinds of affirmations. First, stressing the material, it will say how man shares reality with other objects belonging to the world of space and time. Second, stressing the contrary, it will emphasize the transcendent aspects of human life associated with the spirit. It will say that man is an open, personal, self-conscious subject, and add an observation that human life is constituted in and through personal relationships.

The human person itself possesses a mysterious center of understanding associated with inner forms of self-awareness, insight, judgments, dialogue with truth, goodness, beauty, and unity. One speaks of genuine personal life, freedom, love, responsibility. One seeks to find himself in the context of the whole in a life-and-death struggle. One risks his whole life in the face of meaning. And in risking his life one finds personal freedom.

Man appears to be in such a tension of opposites an embodied spirit. The body is not the life principle; the spirit is not the body; yet each is joined to the other in a living unity. But does the spirit actually transcend the energy of matter? The problematic in any answer remains. Man cannot solve the riddle completely in terms of essence. He is a unity of essence and existence and must work out the final meaning of his nature through committed action. As a living tension of opposites each man must seek to find himself in and through his existence.

Philosophical anthropology works through the method of intellectual insight into meaning. Yet the light always ends in darkness. One is tempted to say that man is imprisoned in his human consciousness.

Religious faith is also an intellectual insight into meaning but extends to man's deeper inward *experience* of a creating and loving Presence. Faith is the light shining in the darkness of human insight; yet it is at the same time man's personal response to the saving Presence and call of God.

A theological anthropology, then, presupposes a philosophical anthropology and attempts to integrate its insights. Each seeks to answer the two basic questions: What is man? What is the meaning of his existence? Each centers attention on man's inner act of existing and his act of self-understanding.

An Historical Perspective

Man has always questioned himself about the mystery of his essence and the meaning of his life. For one to be a man demands that he seeks and accepts responsibility for his person and life.

1. In antiquity man framed the questions and answers about himself and his destiny in image or symbol forms. The images were picture representations associated with the visible world of space and time. In general one spoke within the horizon of a cosmology which considered the heavens and the earth. But the images were always symbols. The pictures pointed beyond themselves to some immanent and transcendent Source, but in the manner of a question. Who fixes and holds up this earth and heaven? What God shall we adore? One observed the creative power and energy found in visible things, but the question remained. What Power rules over the heavens, the earth, and is the lord of man? The answer is given in the form of mystery or dilemma:

No one knows whence creation has arisen;
And whether he has or has not produced it:
He who surveys it in the highest heaven,
He only knows, or haply he may know not.[1]

A person devoid of discrimination, or one perplexed by the delusion of the objects of this visible world, might answer: This world alone exists. There is no other. The wise person, however, turns his attention inward towards his deepest self and inner awareness:

The wise man should merge his speech in his mind, and his mind in his intellect. He should merge his intellect in the Cosmic Mind, and the Cosmic Mind in the Tranquil Self.[2]

The inner perceived or discovered understanding gave rise to primitive societies and cultures. At the same time, man's primitive

---

[1] *Hymn of Creation* (cf. *The Upanishads*, Harper Torchbook, New York, 1963, p. 19).
[2] Katha Upanishad, Ibid., p. 76.

experience of the meaning of human life embraced an awareness of a Holy Mystery. Man expressed this consciousness in cosmic myth stories and public acts of worship.

Primitive man's confrontation with a Holy Mystery became fragmented through association with particular objects, stones, wood, the earth, the heavens, animals, human persons, life functions, and power. Man's deepest experienced meaning raised more problems than solutions. Yet man sought for intellectual insight. Further, religious experience always raised problems of meaning and questioned one's faith.

In the Far Eastern world, answers were given in terms of *self* and the *present moment*. In a psychological peace and openness one seeks and finds a liberation and escape from the intolerable burdens of human life. In the ancient Greek world, answers were given in terms of henotheism, cosmology, and being (metaphysics).

In Hellenic philosophical thought, man was studied from within the horizon of the present visible universe. Answers are given in terms of physics and changing visible nature. What is distinctive about him is his life principle or soul.

For even in the same individual there is succession and not absolute unity: a man is called the same; but yet in the short interval which elapses between youth and age, and in which every animal is said to have life and identity, he is undergoing a perpetual process of loss and reparation—hair, flesh, bones, blood, and the whole body are always changing. And this is true not only of the body, but also of the soul, whose habits, tempers, opinions, desires, pleasures, pains, fears, never remain the same in any one of us, but are always coming and going. And what is yet more surprising is, that this is also true of knowledge; and not only does knowledge in general come and go, so that in this respect we are never the same, but particular knowledge also experiences a like change.[3]

2. A variation in Western philosophical thinking about man can be observed in the rise of *Humanism* in the 14th and 15th centuries. Meister Eckhart (c. 1260-1327) and Nicholas of Cusa (c. 1400-1464) center attention on the importance of the individual person. One confronts truth, Eckhart observes, within the darkness of himself.

[3] Plato, *The Symposium* (cf., *The Works of Plato*, ed. by B. Jowett, New York, p. 338).

This requires that in all your doings you observe the law of truth which is shining eternally in the highest kingdom of your soul. It is the ray or spark of the soul which is giving us counsel all the while, so that you shall pass on to any given person what is an open book to you concerning him, as though all human nature were contained in you and your nature were everybody's nature, you seeing yourself in everyone and everyone in you.[4]

The more one enters into the darkness of his mind, confronting the opposites of intelligence and sensibility, Nicholas of Cusa remarks, the more he perceives that one must seek truth at the juncture where impossibility appears to confront him. In facing the inner limitations of man one confronts the living God, the Absolute Maximum.[5]

The individual person is described in terms of inner personal experience. The secret to the mystery of man is found within his person at the point where one confronts his own limitations. The problem about the mystery of man is perceived within the perspective of the inner depths of the human person.

3. René Descartes (1596-1650) likewise centers his attention on the human person, weighing ideas about the human mind and body against each other. In this situation he raises, once again, the problematic about man. How does one perceive the basic unity in man when his body appears somewhat like a machine and his "I" is experienced as a substance, or essence, existing as a pure spirit, a thinking and conscious ego? Is it true to say, as did Descartes, that the mind is wholly distinct from the body and will continue to be what it is when cut off from the body? Is the human spirit or life principle identified or united with the real and the true? What is the "I" and how is it related to consciousness? What is consciousness and how is it related to the constitution of being or reality?

Descartes attempted to answer from man's subjective experience of his mind, thought, or consciousness, and work outward toward the whole of reality. He seemed to infer that the depths of reality are identified with thought. Man is a concrete example of this

---

[4] cf., *The Nature of Man*, ed. by E. Fromm and R. Xirau. London: Macmillan, 1969, p. 90.
[5] Ibid., p. 98.

29

fact. Man, however, is not pure being but a concrete material thing. One begins to speak of a distinction between man as an extended object (a *res extensa*) and as an intelligent subject (a *res cogitans*). At the same time, one affirms that man is a living, *embodied* subject. Such an emphasis is found in the thinking of Pascal, Kierkegaard, Feuerbach, Marx, and Nietzsche.

5. From a philosophical perspective, the first one to think of a philosophical anthropology was Max Scheler (1874-1928), the German phenomenologist and social philosopher. He fixed his attention on man, on what makes him man, and his experience of the eternal. He undertook a description of the essential fundamentals of human existence in his works: *On the Eternal in Man* (1921), *Forms of Knowledge and Society* (1926), *The Place of Man in the Universe* (1928), and *Man in the Age of Equalization* (1929).

Scheler undertook a searching analysis of the various domains of human existence by an intuitive examination of human experience and a continual rethinking of the meaning of life. He maintained that his method was neither subjectivism nor idealistic but related to hard reality and the common experience of mankind known through history and sociology, religion and psychology.

According to Scheler, human knowledge is never purely subjective or abstract but is always related to reality and the creative process inherent in reality. At times man relates his manner of knowing to particulars. This is the first type of knowledge called, in general, scientific. Such scientific knowledge has for its function human control and mastery. It seeks to give man control over his nature, society, and the future of history.

At times man searches for a knowledge of the essence of reality and the possible categories of essences. Man is ever seeking to lift himself up to a full participation in the whole of reality. The goal of such knowledge is to achieve a living union between his being and that of the deepest reality itself. Such a human search into the essences of things makes man to be himself. This manner of human knowing is the foundation for both metaphysics and the construction of particular sciences.

At times man enters into a living conscious *experience* of reality and its depths. The goal, again, is to achieve a living union between a person and the complicated order of reality together with a living experience of the grounding Absolute. Such a living experience of reality embraces a form of religious awareness. It is existential in nature and goes on from moment to moment. It is related to the human search for the unity of his person and a fullness of life. Hence, as Scheler maintains, the personal form of human existence— indeed the individually personal—extends into the very depth of the world-basis.

In such a framework of man's modes of knowing, we recognize first, our manner of knowing particular empirical objects or events; second, our mode of seeking after and knowing the essence of things; and third, our general human mode of knowing and *experiencing* the whole of reality. This last mode of knowing is an experience we share with all other men, though at the same time it is always uniquely personal. It comprises a synthesis with the other two modes of knowing.

From a scientific viewpoint, man appears to be a psycho-physical object, a concrete acting unit. The goal of man's concrete 'act-center' is direct union between its being and that of reality. The act-center realizes its essential nature and eternalizes its ontic self in such a participation. This suggests that an objective manner of knowing particular objects in this world includes a crucial personal factor which forms the basis of an objective attitude.

A primary feature of man, existing as a psycho-physical object, is that the human subject or person takes the world of his environment to be *the* world, although the specific content varies according to the individual subject or community. What Scheler is saying is that each man confronts the whole of reality within the context of a particular time and place. Such an ontic relativity is a component of every human being. The context of a particular environment includes all existing human structures and institutions. A man

31

becomes who he is, thinks, loves, and finds meaning within his particular world.

Man, however, seeks to transcend and correct such a limited, natural, ontic viewpoint. As a *spiritual* person, the contrasting element in man, he seeks after insights into absolute reality or the essence of the whole. This is man's philosophical manner of knowing, which determines his attitude towards things and his relationships to them. In contrasting these two viewpoints, Scheler speaks of 'scientific' cognition and 'philosophical' cognition.

Philosophical cognition in this sense is a person's manner of knowing rather than a given system of answers. The emphasis is on epistemology, or how the human person knows. When we study man, we perceive that there is an active power in the center of the person which makes him soar to the depths of reality. We come to speak of man's love of essential reality; or, as Scheler declares, there is a love-determined movement of the human person towards participation in the essential reality of all possibles. Man both knows this way and has insights into his knowledge. He seeks to achieve a living participation in essential reality, a participation which excels the knowledge possessed by the person. This second manner of knowing, then, is a direct participation in reality. If the primal essence is *life*, then it is man's seeking after and participation in life. If the primal essence is *love*, then it is man's seeking after and sharing in the activity of love.

Man never ceases thinking in this manner until he comes to the end of the journey in death. Man is a being who ceaselessly seeks to perceive the essence of things, to live, to love. A modern existentialist would say that man's relation to Being is such that he seeks to appropriate it either through action, possession, or attempts to become one with it. Jean-Paul Sartre speaks of this as man's pursuit of Being.

But if man is a being who seeks to know the whole of reality, what insights ground his knowing as he live in the world of space and time? What are man's primal insights?

First, Scheler replies that man living in this world always doubts about something. But this human condition of doubt discloses at the same time man's basic insight: there are some things—there is something—rather than nothing. We know this, experience its truth content, and wonder over and over again. The reality of things and human knowledge are obvious facts; but they are not facts which anyone can take for granted. Each man faces these facts and wonders about the meaning of it all.

As man faces the world of existing things, he comes to a second insight which he expresses in the judgment: there is an absolute Ground to all that is. One may deny this insight and make every manner of intellectual effort to remove it. But in every denial one looks, in fact, through the web of relative entities in the direction of a grounding absolute. Men live and think with the second insight even as they face each day the relative being of all objects belonging to this world of space and time. Yet, in the world of the relative, what is absolute?

The third insight, which follows an order of evidence, can be expressed in the form of a judgment: every entity must necessarily possess an *essence* and an *existence*. Once man perceives the essential content of an object (or an act), or recognizes a particular arrangement of interrelated essences, such knowledge must be distinguished from his knowledge of the realm of relative and contingent existence. The knowledge of a particular essence is in some way *definitive*. One perceives a genuine insight into the whatness of the thing. When one speaks, however of the *existence* of such an essence, he never arrives at more than presumptive truth, certainly dependent on the realities of the future and the findings of later experience. In this context, Scheler is saying that we may affirm something true about the *essence* of man; but having said this, one must perceive the problems inherent in speaking about human *existence*. We can also appreciate why philosophical insight will tend to stress the essence of things and the relationships to an absolute essence.

Man at times has a third manner of knowing and understanding. He enters into a living conscious *experience* of reality and its depths. One enters into a living confrontation with the eternal and the absolute, joined at times with a cry of longing. Such knowledge always has the living form of an event as a person, or a community, fights for the meaning of life and for worth and dignity. The experience may come and go, especially at moments when one is unable to find an answer to his search for meaning.

Scheler maintains that this third type of human knowledge is a form of *religious* consciousness and experience. In his opinion, the God of religion and the world-basis of philosophical knowledge may be identical in reality, but as *intentional objects* they are different in essence. The God of religious consciousness 'is' and lives exclusively in the religious act, not in metaphysical thinking about realities extraneous to religion. The goal of religion is not rational knowledge of the basis of the universe but a life of communion with the absolute personal Mystery, or God. The foundation for all philosophical thought is the human astonishment that anything should exist. This astonishment prompts the inquiry into the nature of reality. Religious knowledge, in contrast, springs from an experience of the personal Ground of man's being as man longs for life and love, a final salvation for himself and all things. In this context, religion is a life and way of salvation.

This difference in the philosophical and religious modes of knowing does not exclude a living connection in the life of the human mind and the basic reality. As Scheler says: the essential peculiarity of the absolute—the reality underlying all things real—must be of necessity that which gives life or salvation to all things, including man. But any such living connection between metaphysics and religion in no way invalidates the basic differences between these two forms of human knowledge and the consequent difference between the principles and procedures by which they develop. Faith in God, or religion, does not live by the grace of metaphysics any more than knowledge of the world-basis lives by the grace of religious experience.

The philosophical anthropology of Scheler depends upon epistemology. Conscious human perception reveals the intelligibility of the visible world of reality and its Ground. The issue is one of perceiving and understanding the total human self in a living relationship to Being and its ultimate Ground. The problem

34

is: Does the human mind perceive and understand the Ground of the visible material universe?

But a further question arises. What does Max Scheler mean when he speaks of the human *person?*

According to the anthropology of Scheler, the human person is a *being* in this world and in confrontation with other human persons directed towards God. A person exists and lives only in the execution of concrete acts. Who the person *is*, is disclosed in and through the life that he creatively lives out. A person reveals himself most deeply in his emotional acts. Loving is the deepest act open to man.

It is man as person who loves, and it is man as person who is discovered in and through love. It is precisely as persons that men are bound together in a loving presence of God. The value disclosed in the movement of love is unique to love. The cognitive element found in this movement constitutes its own mode of evidence. Why this is so must be related to the conscious experience of love which is an unique, immediate, and direct emotional orientation to value. Love constitutes its own reason for being, its own meaning, its own justification. In this sense, the meaning disclosed in the movement of love is unique to love. There is no question of rational proof or demonstration. The meaning of its value can be understood only by being lived.

Love is not blind. Rather, it is a perceptive openness. It allows other objects or persons to be what they are. But love itself is not directed towards this or that but towards wholeness and the fullness of being. Where love is absent, the unique value of an object or person remains veiled.

From such an anthropological viewpoint of love, Scheler perceives that the whole order of reality is one of love. Love is the Ground in and out of which things become what they are. In this context, man emerges and becomes what he is. Through love he discovers who he is and who others are. It is as person, in an open movement of love, that a man discovers that he and his fellow men participate in a community centered in God. God, in such a framework of reality, is the personal love center of the total structure

35

of Being. An order of love discloses the meaning of the world, an order in which both God and men participate freely. Where love is operative, there is always a becoming, a growth, an emergence in the direction of a new fullness. What man is living out concretely in a world with other men is his personal, unique contribution to the meaning of the whole. Living in this world is uniquely human; and it is as a concrete, unique person, and as a free human person, that man participates in the creative loving order of the universe.

5. From the viewpoint of Max Scheler, all the problems in anthropology are related to a central question: What can we *know?* Scheler in answering this question maintains that man has three living modes of knowing: 1) he can and does know concrete things; 2) he can and does know the basic whole of reality; 3) he has a living experience of its grounding creative and loving Presence. Man lives, however, within a visible world of space and time. One is tempted to restrict his viewpoint to this mode of knowing. In general, this is the position of Arnold Gehlen, the German philosopher who studies man from an empirical horizon of knowing in his work: *Man, His Nature and Position in the World* (1952).

Gehlen defines man as a unified subject, an acting essence. At the same time, man is a deficient essence and endeavors to find a perfecting of his essence through action. Through action one makes himself. Through action one builds up himself.

To survive in life and to free himself from anxiety, man creates tools, language, symbol structures of meaning, and a common social environment which he shares with other human beings. Institutions or social patterns of action impart a specific autonomy to the individual persons participating in society. At the same time, Gehlen stresses action as determinant of valid thought, defining truth as man's coherence with fact. Man, however, possesses an inner truth, which is a form of inner acting certainty. The direction of man's acts is towards meaning as he attempts to live in a particular world.

Gehlen, further, recognizes the problems that come to man as he attempts to live and act in a technological society. Such problems, however, can be solved only within some ontological framework.

As a consequence, the investigations of Gehlen have led him towards the acceptance of an idealistic metaphysics. An empirical philosophy of man is an impossibility. A philosophical anthropology is possible only within the horizon of some ontology. The radicalism promised by the viewpoint, "To the things themselves," comes to a dead end with the visible world, as one must still face the open transcendental world of his own person, which is also a fact, a phenomenon of self-consciousness. And this open self-consciousness must still face the problem of obvious meaning disclosed in the things of this world.

6. P. Teilhard de Chardin (1881-1955), in light of the problem which we have just considered, endeavored to relate the world of phenomena to the intelligibility of the whole of reality through a method of analysis and synthesis. Results of such a method are found in his studies: *The Phenomenon of Man* (1938-40) and *Man's Place in Nature* (1949). At the same time, Chardin sought to combine scientific work and Christian effort in the one and same human life. Here he integrated his conscious psychology into an understanding of the whole and produced his work *The Divine Milieu* (1926-27).

When we look at the viewpoint of Chardin, we observe the following guiding principles or suppositions.

1. Chardin is of the opinion that when man observes and studies phenomena, he is engaged in an *analytic* scientific study of reality which leads in a direction away from divine realities.

Deeply rooted in the nature of man as we find him is the conviction that the secret of the universe is found within the world we know and see. Man as we know him seeks to discover the secret of the real.

The first step taken by the scientific mind is to tear the universe to pieces and analyze its elements. The scientific method of inquiry and its conclusions are governed by the principle that the secret of things in this universe lies in their elements. Turning this analysis in the direction of the microscopic, we have disclosed within matter an astonishing series of natural units, colliding particles that are in constant motion, fragments of electric atoms that we can count and weigh and follow the direction of their gravitation. An historical analysis of the past joins hands with such a physico-chemical analysis and leads to the conclusion that everything in the universe is dissolved down to some form of energy. It is impossible to say, however, for lack of analysis, whether the grounding energy is matter. This we do know: Matter, itself, is a specific form of energy.

At the end of such an analytical search have we come closer to the central point of man's inquiry?

Chardin would answer this question in a positive way by saying that scientific analysis leads man to the extreme lower limits of matter. But here the temptation is to affirm that these ultimate particles of matter hold the very essence of the secret of the universe. If this were truly so, we would have to say that science forces us back into materialism. We would have to dismiss any reality called *spirit*, concluding that everything is a plurality of matter and unconsciousness.

But where scientific analysis leads to is nothing but the lower limits of matter. The particles of atoms disappear into a kind of formless energy. In analyzing particles we forget or overlook an ordering principle of intelligibility found in the complexity of the visible material universe. In such a perspective, an analysis of matter leads one to perceive the presence and primacy of a contrary element: spirit.

2. Chardin is of the opinion, then, that objective scientific insight discloses the synthetic structure of the universe. The ordering principle is imponderable and cannot be analyzed. Who can analyze the nature of the life principle in man? Yet it is this transcending principle present in the human body which unifies the complexity of the many particles and organs. If the evolving universe has been successful in bringing man and human thought to birth in an un-

imaginable tangle of chance and mishaps, then there is present, evidence that the universe is fundamentally directed by an energy or power that is eminently in control of the elements that make up the universe. If, then, we look upwards from the lowest level of energy hidden in matter towards man, we perceive by sign the influence of a *spiritual* energy immanent in the whole.

In this perspective, the universe appears as a huge cone, whose base extends into the darkness of the particles of matter, while its apex rises up and concentrates in consciousness objectified in its highest form in man. Throughout the whole, the same creative influence makes itself felt but always in a more conscious, more purified, more complex form. In this sense, the synthetic structure of the universe discloses the principle: All consistence comes from Spirit. In this frame of reference, Chardin thinks cosmic evolution is without an explanation of intelligibility if it is not terminated in a creating Center or Ground: a personal God. The center point— or the Omega Point—seems to be personal, since evolution proceeds in the direction of personal consciousness. This is what is happening in the case of man. To confront these facts or events, there must be a reversal of perspective. Hence, one perceives the presence of freedom, interior experience, personal self-consciousness.

3. The phenomenon of man discloses not a heap of stones held together by inter-fused elements of material energy, but the highest creative reaction in the universe, consisting, as it were, in a collective human consciousness and action in process of development. Such a statement or affirmation made by Chardin does not speak directly of man as a small separate unit isolated from the universe. The content of the statement looks at mankind as a natural phenomenon in the evolutionary process of the universe. Chardin's viewpoint is never to look at man as a single "ego" cut off from the whole of reality. Rather, Chardin looks at mankind in the context of the whole of the universe evolving upwards in the direction of spirit. He looks at man from the viewpoint of totality.

We have difficulties, however, when we look at man as a natural phenomenon and try to comprehend the meaning of the special energies found in him. We tend to look at him from the viewpoint of scientific analysis, and here men appear as unified material energy centers. Biology, for example, says that man is alive but an organic material unit. One is looking at man from the perspective of physics. Often one fails to notice that the unified energy in man comes together in a living person, with freedom, inner experience, and self-consciousness.

But when one changes his direction of thinking and looks in the direction of totality or wholeness, he observes the one immense process: the evolving development of the universe. Here one vast phenomenon is taking place. The meaning of man lies within the phenomenon. Man himself becomes the key which unlocks the door hiding the secrets to the meaning and development of the universe. The evolving universe is attaining its end in living forms of self-consciousness.

As a phenomenon in the universe, the embodied unified living centers which we call man disclose the psychic current of energy hidden in the universe. In the world of man, the psychic factors of self-consciousness and freedom become the principal phenomena. At the same time, this human mass is weaving its way around the world, building a network of communications with shared thought and conversation. The world is being humanized. The phenomenon of evolution seems to have reached its climax in human consciousness as such, and the process appears to be irreversible. What comes to the surface and is disclosed then in man is the imponderable current of spirit. Paradoxically, however, man experiences the intelligibility and meaning of spirit from within. His responsibility is to cooperate actively with his spiritual gifts.

Chardin, of course, does not like to contrast spirit and matter in the universe. Man is embodied spirit; and God enters into creative union with the reality of his creation. There are not two compartments in the universe, the spiritual and the material; they are, rather, two directions found in the evolutionary process: the plurisation of things through matter and a unification of everything. The human life principle is a sign that the evolutionary creative process is moving towards unity. In this context, man is either the demand for, or the anticipation of a later unification of spirit.

This is, in general, Chardin's scientific picture of the universe and of the whole of reality. The twofold movement of the viewpoint is one, first, of *analysis* leading in the direction of material energy; second, of *synthesis* leading in a reverse direction towards totality and the unique ground of things, a personal, immanent, yet transcendent creating Center. The viewpoint is an intuition into the intelligibility or meaning of phenomena. It comprises a study of man as a phenomenon. In this context, the viewpoint leads to an *ontology* rather than to a *metaphysics*. Chardin is not interested in what lies beyond the physical but what is hidden or manifest *within* the universe.

Chardin specifies this ontological viewpoint through an added or integrated psychological experience (he will say that he believes it through love and necessity) and a Christian religious experience. From his Christian viewpoint he considers Jesus Christ to be the divine *Logos*, or the immanent yet transcendent creating Principle of the universe.

Chardin thought, finally, that many modern men—even outside Christianity—were living and thinking within the framework of such a viewpoint.

7. Chardin's viewpoint was based on scientific inference. Yet we observe the importance of psychological experience. His love for the universe gave him a deep interior confidence. If his picture of the whole had been shattered by evidence, he would have felt lost and despairing. This aspect brings us to the viewpoint of Martin Buber (1878-1956) which he called "psychologizing of the world." An independent, yet similar, expression of thought can be found in the philosophy of Gabriel Marcel and Ferdinand Ebner.

The intelligibility we give or find in the universe, Martin Buber says, does not exist outside of our person but within and in the context of personal life. Over and over again our lives give testimony to the meaning we find in this world. This essential is my *I* facing the world. At the same time, the world faces and confronts me; and within this basic relationship the real happens. I am not the universe. The universe or world is not I, though there is a connection of a relation. Human thought brings the world into the human mind or soul. Cosmic phenomena are grasped in a psychic manner. On the other side, man is a thing or a person in the world. He appears as its product, understandable on the basis of an evolutionary process. In such a context, we come to the problem of man.

Buber answers the questions touching the problem of man from what man *knows*.[6] Man is given to himself as a subject. The person is man in his wholeness. One experiences his humanity in a inner awareness and in a manner distinct from his experience of any other object. In this experience one reflects upon himself as a person.

It is proper to man, says Buber, to face himself as a problematic and to ask the question: What is man? This question can be asked and answered only in the context of one's personal life. One must expose himself in everything he can meet when he is really living. In this sense, the wholeness of the answer is never completely given in life. Yet, in each man the problematic of being is stated in terms of life. Added to this, Buber agrees with Scheler in maintaining that we live in an age in which man has become fully and thoroughly problematic to himself. He no longer knows what he essentially is, and he knows that he does not know. Nevertheless, each man out of the experience of his life gives testimony to an answer.

The answer to the question, What is man? is given by Buber in the context of man's living relationships with the world, with other human persons, with the Mystery of the Absolute, God. A human person brings his nature and historical situation to a fullness of meaning to the extent that he is open to these relationships. A person destroys himself and loses meaning in his life by closing himself off.

First, Buber maintains man must enter into a living relationship

---

6 Cf., Martin Buber, "On the Psychologizing of the World," in *Philosophy Today* (Winter 1967) vol XI, no. 4/4, p. 227-232; *I-Thou*. New York: Scribners, 2nd ed., 1958; *Between Man and Man*. London: Kegan Paul, 1947.

with the world. I face the world and the world faces me; between us the real happens. This essential basic relationship gives meaning to human life. The relationship is injured when one forgets or overlooks non-psychic nature, or when one's relationship with the world closes off his proper relationships with other human persons and the absolute Thou. Through a living relationship with the world, or being, one is able to possess the universe as an idea; but what is essential to the universe does not enter into the idea. In this relationship one can perceive that the human soul is not the universe. Rather, the human life principle, or soul, confronts the world. What is essential to the soul is not included in the world.

In confronting the real, man experiences himself to be one thing. He is not a duality of body and soul. At the same time man experiences two contrary aspects in himself by which he is able to say that he is an embodied soul or an embodied spirit. I perceive myself through bodily senses while I am conscious of my person in a manner that transcends the senses.

We are inclined to take the edge off human dying by saying or implying that the duality in man comes apart in death and the soul lives on. We know, however, only that death ends our journey through this world. It is possible to say that the human person perceives that he will live on beyond death. Such a living hope is in man. Yet death is a mystery and what takes place in death takes place in mystery.

One can speak of man as embodied soul or as an embodied spirit. To say that man is an embodied *soul* refers to a living relationship between the man and his body. The soul may be said to give life to the body. But to say that man is an embodied *spirit* refers to a living relationship between man and the Being that does not disclose itself in the world and does not enter into the worldly manifestation. In such a context soul and spirit are not to be understood as the individual person, the I, but refer rather to a living relationship between the personal I and worldly or non-worldly being. The spirit in man is inclined to bend back towards itself and to forget that it is grounded in a mystery which lies beyond itself. Man is tempted to think on a plane of relationship between

43

man and the world and to overlook the transcending Ground. Buber says that this situation is the true Fall of man; and here the Fall takes place. Wholeness is fragmented.

Man's second essential relationship is a living openness towards other human persons. As Buber would say, the fundamental fact of human existence is man with man. When imaginings and illusions are over, a man discovers and experiences what it is to be human in his meetings with his fellow-man. He must be truly open and break through to other human persons. There are genuine human relations only between persons.[7]

The fundamental fact of human existence is, from such a viewpoint, neither the individual or some collective aggregate. Man is really human in so far as he steps, with full responsibility, into living relationship with other individual persons. Language is a sign and means for such a meeting. Every achievement of the spirit has been incited by it. Man is made man by such encounters. Not only do such meetings unfold and develop, they also decay and wither away. Yet it is rooted in man's nature that he should, and must, turn towards other human persons and enter into dialogue and communion with them.

Such human encounters are happenings which disappear in the moment of their appearance, disclosing the pathos of human solitude and tragedy. One man is not another man; and each human person is opposed to the other in his nature, disclosing to each an irreconcilable opposition of being.

Buber maintains, then, that the essence of man can be known only in and through man's living relations. Further, a person's bonds with his generation and his society are of his essence, and we must know what these bonds really mean if we want to know the essence of man. "Consider man with man, and you see human life, dynamic, twofold, the giver and the receiver, he who does and he who endures, the attacking force and the defending force, the nature which investigates and the nature which supplies information, the request begged and granted—and always both together,

---

[7] Buber, *Between Man and Man*, p. 202-5.

completing one another in mutual contribution, together showing forth man. Now you can turn to the aggregate and you recognize it as man according to the fulness of relation which he shows."[8]

Man's third essential relation is his encounter with the Absolute, the Personal Mystery, or God. "We may come nearer the answer to the question what man is when we come to see him as the eternal meeting of the One with the Other." Buber takes it as a guiding principle of human existence that man is addressed by God in his life and that the life of man is meant by God to have a fullness of meaning. Our responsibility is to be open and aware of 'the signs' that continually address us in everything that happens. Human life means being addressed, and the signs of address are the events that happen to us each day, again and again. "What occurs to me addresses me."

I know no fulness but each mortal hour's fulness of claim and responsibility. Though far from being equal to it, yet I know that in the claim I am claimed and may respond with responsibility, and know who speaks and demands a response.

I do not know much more. If that is religion then it is just everything, simply all that is lived in its possibility of dialogue. Here is space also for religion's highest forms. As when you pray you do not thereby remove yourself from this life of yours but in your praying refer your thought to it, even though it may be in order to yield it; so too in the unprecedented and surprising, when you are called upon from above, required, chosen, empowered, sent, you with this your mortal bit of life are referred to, this moment is not extracted from it, it rests on what has been and beckons to the remainder which has still to be lived, you are not swallowed up in a fulness without obligation, you are willed for the life of communion.[9]

A man finds himself in finding God, yet at the same time he must find himself to be truly open to God; and in being open to God he must be open to the world and his fellow men. Man is a mystery and a problem to each man. No one, then, from Buber's understanding, can fully answer the question: What is man? Rather, each human person discovers and finds himself, from moment to moment, as he is truly open to the world, to his fellow human beings, and to the call of the absolute personal mystery.

---

[8] Ibid., p. 205.
[9] Ibid., p. 14.

45

The Problematic of Method

With the background of such an historical perspective one can perceive that problems arise constantly about the specific nature of a philosophical anthropology. For example, the question is raised: What *method* should one follow in arriving at a coherent body of knowledge about man and what is the *content* of the basic insights?

One point of view seeks to start from particular empirical data— from biology, from historical studies of man's origins, from psychology, sociology, culture, or the history of religions—and then integrates the significance of particular facts into a general picture of man. The other viewpoint starts with man's self-understanding and experience in a social and historical context.

The first method raises the questions: Does the empirical data discovered through observation allow one to come to some general and unified synthesis? What are the principles or suppositions which give one insight into the nature of man and the meaning of his life? Some significance must be found in particular facts and applied to a particular human person and the whole of mankind.

The second method places the emphasis on man's self-understanding and human experience. Such a procedure also raises particular questions. Can one really arrive at a genuine understanding of the nature of man and the meaning of human life? Are such insights no more than subjective assumptions? Are personal insights of understanding related to concrete facts and events? How can one arrive at a wholeness of understanding that is related to the significance of particular events and facts?

Such problems about method direct attention towards the two basic questions about man: Who am I? What is the meaning of my existence? Here we may make the following observations.

1. These questions cannot be answered directly by empirical science. Empirical science focuses its attention on some observed part of man, some fact, some event. The center of attention is always an object rather than man as a living personal subject. We cannot know man by collecting a group of isolated facts or events. At some point a human person must experience what it means to

be a man. Yet this is not the total answer. What matters in empirical science is what has significance in disclosing the meaning of some whole. Any occurrence, when deeply understood for what in fact it is, is revelatory of how the world is and how the whole of reality is. Thus every fact about man has some significance and importance. There are no bare facts without significance. In such a context it must be said: Phenomena disclose meaning.

2. The study of man's primitive origins and development can never succeed of itself in answering the basic questions. Descriptions of becoming can never answer the questions of essence and nature. Yet every moment has its own significance and that significance can be related to the significance of every other moment and the total movement of man's historical journey and development. Again, it must be said: Phenomena disclose meaning.

3. Philosophical anthropology is the study of man from the perspective of man's total act of existing. In this sense the basic problems of man, when answered, must be related to human experience in its widest sweep, in a living relationship to reality. Such an effort at self-understanding proceeds by way of insight and extended search into the intelligibility of self, human consciousness, conscience, thinking, speaking, loving, and acting in the world within which the experience is perceived. These insights, in turn, are placed within the circle of some whole, some horizon of ultimate meaning. The insights are not pure *a priori* perceptions; rather, they are based on self-experience associated with human consciousness and self-understanding. The insights are integrated into a whole which is changed or modified through added insights.

4. Philosophical anthropology has a vision of reality, an ontology. One understands the meaning of human existence within the context of the whole. Each moment of human experience has some significance and importance. They are no bare human facts without meaning; every moment has its significance and that significance is related to the significance of every other moment and the total movement of the whole.

The way in which man philosophizes about himself as man is far from indulging in some idealistic, abstract thought. Rather, it is the pondering of the intelligibility of every given occasion. A generalizing is undertaken by intuition, with a continual reference made to each new moment to determine whether the generalizing still remains valid or true. In this sense the meaning of each human moment manifests the transcendental aspects of human existence. The phenomena disclose the reality.

5. The elements, then, for philosophical anthropology are both *phenomenological* and *transcendental*. Phenomenology considers the reality and significance of human acts. The transcendental points to the infinite. In this context, the intelligibility of man has meaning only in reference to the non-finite. Yet the last word is never spoken or the last insight obtained. The fundamental phenomena of human existence are allowed to disclose themselves in and through human self-understanding and self-experience. Phenomena tend to disclose the significance of reality. At the same time, the meaning associated with man tends to disclose itself in a tension of opposites: matter and spirit, life and death, meaning and non-meaning, finite and infinite. The tension can be reconciled only in the context of the presence of an immanent yet transcendent personal Mystery. All the transcendent tendencies and insights in man point towards such a Ground of reality.

Chapter 3

Theological Anthropology

The Human Dimensions of Theology

Theology, strictly speaking, is man's reflection upon God's creating and loving Presence. The term *Theology* means man's word about the divine. Yet, having said this, we notice two basic characteristics of theology. First, it is a human effort. Second, man always seeks and finds God in relation to himself and other men.

It is a human effort. The person who does the perceiving and reflecting is always man. It is always a human inquiry and takes its place among the other human works of man. The insights, the images or representations, the affirmations, are always events of human action. Further, in theology, one always speaks out of a position of self-understanding in relation to reality. Even when we say that theology speaks in a context of what a community believes and professes, the subject of the speaking and professing is always man. Theology can and will speak of divine answers, but what it gives out of its human effort are human answers.

At the same time, man always seeks and finds God in relation to himself and other men. As far as man is concerned, God must always be known and experienced humanly. In theology a living relationship between God and man is always implied. And once you say this, then it is necessary to look at the other term—man— and ask the questions: What is man? How does he interpret the meaning of human existence? As a consequence, it is said: Anthropology is the *source* of theology. One comes to focus attention on the transcendental tendencies found in man.[1]

---

[1] cf., *Mysterium Salutis*, Einsiedeln: Benziger, 1967, Vol. 2, 406ff.

Man as the Source of Theology

Man experiences within himself a dynamism towards an absolute in act, meaning, truth and life. This datum of human experience is the basis for defining man as an embodied spirit, or a being open to the infinite. We give a determination to man's nature from the openness he experiences within himself. We are specifying in reference to man himself. We are looking at man and what he experiences. But what grounds this openness found in man? What does it mean and imply? What is its end purpose?

The picture of man is altered if we answer all these questions in relation to God. We end up by defining man in a living reference to God. We are now saying: God is the creating ground of all that man is and does. Man's personal existence has meaning only in a final reference to God. Man's end purpose is as a partner in a dialogue. Man stands under God's call. The openness found in man is oriented towards hearing God's word addressed to him. Man no longer stands alone. God is always in the picture as the creating Spirit and the loving Thou.

Theological anthropology states that all that man is and does has a living relation to God. Man is defined in terms of such a relationship. Man never exists in himself. All he is has its foundation in God's Spirit. Man never exists apart from God. Man is never independent of a living relationship with God. Man can never live just for himself. This is why man is always raising the question of God. All that man is involves the question: What is the *ground* of my existence?

We are now able to see why man is the source of theology. All of his questions are stages on the way to his knowledge and mysterious encounter with God. Man in some real manner labors to become what he must be. He has a drive within him to achieve an open break-through to what gives him full wholeness in being human. He searches, day after day, for the Ultimate, the Sacred, the Holy, the Transcendent. Under this aspect, theology is an explanation of what-I-am and what-I-am-doing. At the same time, it is also a reflecting service. It struggles to help man identify himelf. It seeks to address itself to what is happening in a religious community. It labors to give intelligibility to a shared human experience of being human and religious. It searches to find new language, to speak with meaning to new modes and forms of human knowledge and self-awareness.

If man must seek and find himself in his living relationship with God, another aspect of the encounter must be stated. The knowability of his creating and loving Presence in and among men is bestowed on man as God's favor or grace. God himself is man's life and peace. God gives himself to man as a gift, though it must be received and accepted. Here, however, one must add: God is truly known by man in a fullness when He is meaningful to man in his human existence.

The Transcendental Dimensions of Man's Nature

We define man, as we have seen, as a unity of opposites or contraries, an embodied spirit. To define man this way discloses the presence of opposites in his total human activity.

Man is a material object in a visible world of space and time. In his truly human activity man orders his activity towards his body, towards living in this world with its related objects, towards the present moment. His self-awareness and understanding are always related to his body and the visible world. One seeks to grasp the intelligibility of reality in relation to the material and visible.

Yet, the transcending factor of *spirit* is always present and at work. We come to speak of man as an *open* being. He seeks by nature to break out of the world of space and time through transcending personal experiences, insights, and tendencies. In this sense man is open to the totality of reality in the depths of his person. The horizon of his knowing is infinite. He is open to the Absolute. This openness is extended to his personal relations with other human persons. Men seek after a shared, open experience. A closed-in self-understanding is narrow, shallow, inhuman.

The transcendent openness found in man, together with his experience and insights, becomes the means by which we face and

question man's awareness of a holy, personal Presence and Mystery
The intelligibility of man's religious experience, however, must
always be related to the opposite tension in man: his body. In this
context, man experiences that he is being addressed or called in
keeping with the concrete conditions of time and place. We are
able to say that God calls to man in his concrete history and
through particular events. The evidence is man's living experience;
and the living experience is always a living relation. Man, again,
will represent or picture out the thematic content of his experience.
He will speak of a personal presence and address, but with images
and ideas associated with the experience of his body.

When one defines man as an embodied spirit, he raises the question and problem of transcendental anthropology. Since man is an
embodied spirit, the question is placed as long as man is what he
is. Man, when he answers, faces the problem of himself and his
experiences through a transcendent determination, his personal
freedom. We say that man is a spiritual subject. It is possible to
answer in terms associated with the body. One is always free to say
that man's living encounter with God is only a psychic process.
One may be only talking to the various strata of the self.

The decisive event, then, is God's immediate self disclosure to the
human person. The final answers to the transcendental dimensions
found in man must come from this self-mediating Presence.

But why cannot philosophy say all of this through pure intellectual insight rather than having a theology refer to the total human
experience, part of which is pre-conceptual? The answer is found
in an obvious fact. God in revealing himself to each man always
conceals himself. The hidden, immanent, and transcendent Ground
of what man is, is experienced to be a personal Mystery. Man
experiences that he is confronted by a personal Ground, addressed
through the medium of a Word (the Logos), in a form of dynamic
power and love (the Spirit). Man infers this from his total human
experience. The medium of the encounter or the dialogue is a self-
understanding experience rather than pure intellectual insight. The
hiddenness is completely incomprehensible. Truth is given in and
through a mysterious Presence.

1. Primitive man expressed the deepest meaning of who and what he was in forms of religious response, representations, and socialization. In general, he objectified the perceived meaning in and through his *nature gods.*

In ancient China man understood himself in relation to the laws of heaven and earth. The whole of the universe was viewed in a microcosm-macrocosm form. In ancient India man understood himself within a framework of a law of social duty and the wheel of rebirths (karma-samsara). Often, as in Mesopotamia, Egypt, and Rome, though man fragmented the mystery of the holy Other, one explained the meaning of human existence in terms of function associated with a divine-human continuum. Personification and concrete picturing gave man a personal reference to help him perceive what his religious experience pointed to. Mythology, or the stories of the gods, supplied concrete imagery for the laws of nature and accounted for the presence of the good as an ordering cosmic force. Goodness is a principle working in the actual world. Justice reigns in the world of the gods. The cosmic order both respects and requires justice. "The character of our present life, which is said to be under Zeus, you know from your own experience."[2]

Judaism and Christianity, as is obvious from the Old and New Testament writings, speak within a framework of a theological anthropology. Man is made in the image of God. "So God created man in his own image, in the image of God he created him" (Gen. 1. 27). Like God, man is a creating personal presence. "You have given him dominion over the works of your hands; you have put all things under his feet" (Ps. 8. 6). The meaning of human existence receives an answer in terms of God's loving presence. "You, O Lord, have not forsaken those who seek you" (Ps. 9. 10). Man's personal relationship with God must extend itself outward to one's neighbor. "You shall love your neighbor as yourself" (Lev. 19. 18).

Yet, the Bible contains no organized explanation of man. It

[2] Plato, *Statesman.*

speaks only of man's perceived meaning of human life in this world

2. Origen (c. 185-c. 254), the first systematic theologian in the Christian community, did offer a unified explanation of the mystery of man in his *First Principles*. He wrote from a Christian and Platonic viewpoint. This means that Origen speaks of man in terms of his understanding of the universe.

What is the divine creating Principle of all things? Origen answers in the thought pattern of Platonism. The creating Principle of all things is the divine Word, or Logos. But he immediately Christianizes the Principle. Jesus Christ is the Logos, the foundation of all things (First Principles, Bk I, Preface). This divine Word is pure Power or Energy, an emanation in and out of God (the Father). The Logos is the Son of God and the Wisdom of God hypostatically existing (Bk I, ch. 2). Through the Logos as a mediating Principle, God creates, establishes, and preserves all things. In man, the Logos is the source of human life and knowledge. At the same time, the Logos draws all men towards goodness, being the Principle of man's justice, sanctification, and redemption.

All men, Origen maintains, are called to a free service of the divine Logos incarnate in Jesus. Such a service is a human life of happiness, goodness, and wisdom. In this sense, "Our subjection to Christ implies the salvation proceeding from Christ" (*Ibid.*, Bk I, ch. 6). The denial of God's rule over man constitutes the Fall of Adam. To the contrary, man's free subjection to the incarnate Logos becomes man's life of salvation. This new life is a living participation in the divine nature.

Following Platonic ideas, Origen spoke of the pre-existence of the human soul and assumed that eventually each man would find life in God. The use of these thoughts allowed Origen to withstand the Valentinian doctrine of natural inequality and the accusations that God, as Creator, is unjust.

3. Similar efforts at constructing a basic theological anthropology can be found in the work of Tertullian, *De Anima* (c. 210 A.D.). The origin of the life principle in man, the soul, comes from a

divine inbreathing rather than from an emanation out of matter (ch. 1), even though the infusion of the soul into man is related to the generating act of the parents (chs. 23-41). This last aspect has come to be known as Traducianism. Tertullian resorted to such a theory in an attempt to explain the habitual condition found in man called Original sin. For Tertullian, further, the soul has a real living relationship to matter, an element of corporality (ch. 9). As a consequence, both rational and non-rational aspects are found in the soul.

Further, there are found in man natural tendencies which turn him towards deliberate sin. These tendencies are passed on from generation to generation. The story of Adam and Eve discloses the basic human situation. As a consequence, every human person is born in the image of Adam and reborn to Christ through Baptism (ch. 40). Some men may be said to be good; others are truly evil; yet all men possess the same basic nature. "There is some good in the worst of us, and the best of us harbor some evil. God alone is without sin, and the only sinless man is Christ, since he is God" (ch. 41. no. 3).

Death, says Tertullian, is a debt we owe to human nature. Everyone born signs this contract. The purpose of death is to separate the soul from its body (ch. 51). Through death the soul escapes from the veil of the flesh into power and light. The soul, itself, is immortal and indivisible. With death the soul passes to a higher life, somewhat like a man awakening from sleep or passing out of a shadow into a better light. There will be a resurrection of the dead and the human body will have a state corresponding to the human acts performed in this world. Those who die in Christ will find eternal life in Christ.

Beyond such general statements, Tertullian observes, men may speculate, but wise men will be unable to answer.

Tertullian experiences the meaning of man from within a world to which he belongs. This world is Christian in outlook, Platonic and Gnostic. He tends to oppose matter and spirit.

4. A similar dualism is to be found in the anthropological opinions of St. Augustine (354-430). Obviously man is one reality but an

emphasis is placed on the spirituality of the human soul. The soul is not a body but spirit (*non sit corpus, sed spiritus*). The soul is not imprisoned in the body as Plato would say; rather, there is a natural inclination in the soul to live in its body. The soul is a spiritual substance. On earth it uses the body. The union of the body and soul makes one man (*unus homo*). The soul itself is a spiritual substance present to all the parts of the human body.

Augustine rejected the idea of the Gnostics that the soul was an emanation out of the spiritual substance of God. He also rejected the material traducianism implied in the thought of Tertullian. His inclination was to accept a form of spiritual traducianism. Considering many hypotheses to explain the origin of the human soul, Augustine concluded that God created the soul of the first man (Adam) directly and at the moment it was united to its proper body. But how does one explain the origin of each human soul? This question disturbed Augustine throughout his entire life. He would have liked to have said that each human soul is created by God directly; but because of his thought that original sin was passed on by each generation, he was inclined to think that some spiritual germ was passed on by the parents to the children. But what is this spiritual germ or *ratio seminalis*? Was it alive, associated with intelligence, or just some energy or power? Augustine asked himself the question throughout his life, and at the end confessed that he did not know.

When St. Augustine was thinking of the origin of the human soul in each human person, his perspective included an interpretation of the Fall of Adam found in the Old Testament. According to his viewpoint, shared with the Catholic community of North Africa, the first human pair were endowed with a state of original justice. This first condition of man included the perfection of body, spirit, and free will. With the Fall of man's first parents, mankind as a whole finds himself in a wounded state. This condition is passed on or transmitted through physical generation. As a consequence, children are baptized *in remissionem peccatorum*.

At the same time Augustine spoke of man as the image of God and maintained that man is grounded in God, knows and loves through his Presence, and experiences the living God. The human mind comes to truth because the spirit of man confronts God within. The human mind knows God exists.

5. The dualism and pessimism found in the theology of St. Augustine continued to find a living expression in Western Christian thought and reached a crucial importance in the theology of Martin Luther (1483-1546).

Man has a twofold nature, a spiritual and a bodily. According to the spiritual nature, which men call the soul, he is called a spiritual, or inner, or new man; according to the bodily nature, which men call the flesh, he is called a carnal, or outward, or old man, of whom the Apostle writes in 2 Cor. 4, "Though our outward man is corrupted, yet the inward man is renewed day by day." Because of this diversity of nature the Scriptures assert contradictory things of the same man, since these two men in the same man contradict each other, since the flesh lusts against the spirit and the spirit against the flesh (Gal. 5).[3]

Again, following a viewpoint of St. Augustine, Luther spoke of two worlds and two kingdoms.

We set forth two worlds, as it were, one of them heavenly and the other earthly. Into these we place these two kinds of righteousness, which are distinct and separated from each other. The righteousness of the Law is earthly and deals with earthly things, by it we perform good works. But as the earth does not bring forth fruit unless it has first been watered and made fruitful from above—for the earth cannot judge, renew, and rule the heavens, but the heavens judge, renew, and rule the earth, so that it may do what the Lord has commanded—so also by the righteousness of the Law we do nothing even when we do much, we do not fulfill the Law even when we fulfill it. Without any merit or work of our own, we must first be justified by Christian righteousness, which has nothing to do with the righteousness of the Law or with earthly and active righteousness. But this righteousness is heavenly and passive. We do not have it ourselves, we receive it from heaven. We do not perform it, we accept it by faith, through which we ascend beyond all laws and works. "As, therefore, we have borne the image of the earthly Adam," as Paul says, "let us bear the image of the heavenly one" (1 Cor. 15.49), who is a new man in a new world, where there is no Law, no sin, no conscience, no death, but perfect joy, righteousness, grace, peace, life, salvation, and glory.[4]

---

[3] Martin Luther, *A Treatise on Christian Liberty* (A Compend of Luther's Theology), Philadelphia: Westminster Press, 1943, p. 77.
[4] Martin Luther, *Lectures on Galatians, 1535*, St. Louis: Luther's Works, 1963, Vol. 26, p. 8.

In the Middle Ages, as we notice in the case of Martin Luther, man was considered within the perspective of a cosmology. The heavens pointed to the world of God and spirit; the earth pointed to the world of man and his secular efforts. Such a perspective failed to do justice to the unity of man's nature. Christian truth falls into the human situation like rain from the sky. The world of God, man, and the earth were static, fixed realities. Little was thought or said about the existential aspects of human life. No one thought to analyze a fundamental human experience found in each human person, the gift and ambiguity of human existence, man's experience of meaning and non-meaning, his total experience of the Holy, his struggle for life even in the midst of death. The importance of God's immediate, creating, and loving Presence in man was not emphasized. No one seemed to realize the importance of the open, transcendental experience associated with man's life. No one noticed how all men, both in the East and the West, had the same common experience of the problem of human existence united to an awareness of a Holy Mystery. One did speak at times of an acting intelligence in man, the *intellectus agens*. One did say that this acting intelligence was a light or *lumen*; but no one seemed to understand that this acting light in man is a transcending *experience* associated with a personal awareness.

Man's interest in himself as a conscious subject begins in modern times with René Descartes (1596-1650). In the act of existing man is conscious of himself as a knowing subject. Further, man has within himself the principle of self-certitude. Yet the dualism remains. Man is a thinking thing (*res cogitans*) and an extended thing (*res extensa*) united through the energy of God.

6. A radical change takes place in the 18th and 19th centuries. Man becomes a problem to himself. There arises, as a result, the beginnings of modern anthropology. We are able to situate the problem of man with the question raised by Immanuel Kant (1724-1804): What can man know? Out of this question arises the other question: Who or What is man?

In such a situation of doubt we recognize today the importance of G. Hegel's *Phenomenology of Mind* which was circulated in the form of notes in 1806. Hegel was attempting to answer Kant's *Critique of Pure Reason* by affirming that man can have an awareness of reality that transcends the physical. The answer given by Hegel was a theological anthropology.

Man is a concrete unity, yet a living tension of opposites, an embodied spirit. Knowledge comes to man in and through his consciousness and enters it as truth. He represents or pictures out his self-experience of reality through his ideas or *Vorstellungs*.

God is the Absolute Spirit, a living, active self-consciousness.[5] He is pure self-existence who empties himself of himself in creating things opposite to himself. Yet God is present and at home in the opposite. Man on his part can be conscious of God's presence within himself through the mediation of experience. The believing mind sees, feels, and hears the dynamic presence of the Spirit. Such an awareness is actual in the believer. It does not start from thought and combine some notion of God with human existence. Rather, it starts from immediate present existence and recognizes the presence of God. Yet, there is something about God that remains concealed and alien to man. In some mysterious way God is Other. Nevertheless, in experiencing this otherness of God, man perceives that God is self-existence (Being-for-Self) and Being for another (the Trinity and creation), yet always at home with itself.

In answer to Kant, then, Hegel maintains that God is known to man in and through his religious consciousness. This experience knows God to be dynamic Spirit, Thought, pure Essence, real Existence. Creation and human existence are opposite dynamic realities. The Spirit of God is always Other. "It is just this that revealed religion knows."

7. In 1927, Martin Heidegger's *Being and Time* appeared. This work was an analysis of actual human existence. The emphasis is on embodiment. Man is an embodied act of existing, caught in

---

[5] It is difficult to say whether Hegel identified the spirit in man with the Absolute Spirit, or with God. The question becomes: Was he a Pantheist? Certainly for Hegel the human spirit is grounded in God, but I do not think he was a Pantheist. At least, he was not a Pantheist towards the end of his life, as one can ascertain by reading his *Lectures on the Philosophy of Religion.*

the conditions or the web of a particular time and place. Heidegger makes no attempt to overthrow the assumption of Kant's *Critique of Pure Reason* that human concepts are pictured out or represented in symbol words associated with space and time. Heidegger accepts such an affirmation as true. Further, Heidegger also perceives the difficulty of man's thinking and affirming in the context of *subject and object*, saying for example, "The sky *is* blue." Obviously, the sky *is blue* only in some living relationship with a human subject with a particular kind of eyes. When man thinks and affirms in the framework of subject and object, problems of intelligibility appear. "Here we have an average kind of intelligibility, which merely demonstrates that this is unintelligible. It makes manifest that in any way of comporting oneself towards entities as entities— even in any Being towards entities as entities—there lies *a priori* an enigma."[6]

Heidegger, in *Being and Time*, seeks to avoid the dilemma of *subject-object* by turning attention toward man's personal act of existing. Each man confronts a strange world of objects. He is thrown into a particular world of entities. Yet no man exists simply within a system of things and objects. Rather, in a man's total act of existing, the intelligibility of the whole of reality (ontology) is being disclosed. With Heidegger there is a change always from the *Ego cogito* of Descartes towards an *I act*.

Human life is a kind of being, a mode of existing. It is accessible to each human person in his lived experience. "The human analytic raises the ontological question of the Being of the 'sum.' "[7]

Heidegger, as we can see, speaking in the context of the studies of Wilhelm Dilthey and Max Scheler, focuses attention on man's total experience. Man, from the evidence of phenomena, is certainly a unit of body and spirit. But what such phenomena point to becomes hidden in mystery since man is thrown into a finite and visible world of space and time.

What we must notice, however, is that man confronts reality

---

[6] Martin Heidegger, *Being and Time*, London: SCM Press, 1962, p. 23, no. 4.
[7] cf., *Being and Time*, paragraph 10, p. 71-77, and paragraph 77, p. 449-56.

and the moaning of human existence in and through a personal lived experience.

Here, of course, the question arises: What is the full dimension of such an experience? Heidegger does not know; perhaps, he says, man can only wait for the answer.

We do perceive, however, says Heidegger, that the human *person* centers man's nature and activity. The 'sum' or the *I am*, is a lived experience of self-awareness, understanding, reflection, and self-activity. And it is in and through this center that man interprets the meaning of reality at every present moment, though confronting the mystery of the whole.

From the perspective of contemporary Catholic theology, it is the meaning and purpose associated with man's open or transcendent consciousness and insight which allow him to experience intelligibility in his religious awareness and responses—being called by a Thou and answering, being chosen and choosing, being encountered through a creating Love and reacting with a grateful communion.

Man's personal, total, living experience grounds theology.

Theology of Human Existence

Protestant theology to a large extent tends to ground its affirmations in God's saving presence and address. It will say: Through God alone can God be known. Catholic theology, for the most part, seeks after a more coherent position. It tends to perceive the wholeness of things. It maintains that God is never known directly but always through some *mediating principle*: creation or reality, historical events, or human experience associated with insight and reason. In such a perspective, it takes creation seriously, as well as history and metaphysics. It proceeds through a method of self-understanding but in a living relationship with reality.

Following such a method of procedure, it makes the affirmations:

First, the whole of reality appears to be dynamic. We term the total, visible universe, creation, perceiving its active dynamism. Creation appears to be grounded in a creative energy undergoing a process of evolution. The temptation, always present throughout a man's life, is to think that the grounding energy is materially some form of electricity. Such a perspective is, of course, material monism. Modern science and mathematics think and work within a framework of material quantities.

Yet, physical science is unable to specify the nature of the grounding energy. What men of science know is appearances. All they seek is what appears to be. What is, is always found in some intelligible form; what appears, is illusive, subject to a continual creative process. At no point is there chaos, or lack of order. Complete or pure chaos would have to be nothingness.

Further, the creative process is always new and fresh. One type of order appears, develops into a variety of possibilities, then decays. But when one form of order decays, a new order appears. At the same time, one form of order is coordinated into one universe.

In so far as the universe appears to be an ordered whole, the grounding principle can be intuited to be a creating, immanent yet transcendent, personal Act of Spirit. Yet this is said in the face of mystery. What each man faces with his self-understanding and experience is a dynamic creative process. Yet, in our darkness, it would seem unreasonable to use the part (the energy) as a weapon against the coherent whole.

Second, the intelligibility of the creative process comes to a living form of self-awareness in man; while the direction of the evolutionary process appears centered in the creation and shared human history of man. The self-consciousness of man indicates a law of spiritualization at work in the universe. The culmination point is the conscious self-knowledge, love, and trust found in and among all men. It was in this context that Teilhard de Chardin wrote:

Mankind, the spirit of the earth, the synthesis of individuals and peoples, the paradoxical conciliation of the whole, and of unity with multitude—all these are called Utopian and yet they are biologically necessary. And for them to be incarnated in the world all we may well need is to imagine our power of loving developing until it embraces the total of men and of the earth.[8]

Third, a man questions himself about who he is; and the answer

---

[8] Teilhard de Chardin, *The Phenomenon of Man* (Harper, 1961), p. 265.

given can come only from a living dynamic of self-awareness. From this manner of knowing we are able to define man as an embodied spirit open to the infinite.

From an empirical or scientific viewpoint, man appears to be an organic unit, or as Scheler says, a psycho-physical object, a concrete acting unit. But conceding such a viewpoint associated with man's sense perception yet starting from empirical evidence, man experiences himself to be an embodied dynamic spirit, a presence open towards transcendence or the infinite. He is one thing, not two. He comes to consciousness in and through the body yet always in and through a transcending act. He seeks and finds himself through a spiritualization process which, in paradox, seems contrary to matter. The spirit, as such, is not experienced as being a thing but a transcending, dynamic, self-awareness or presence, which gives life to the body. In such a context, man through an empirical self-awareness experiences himself to be an embodied spirit.

Fourth, it is in and through such a transcending act of spirit that man comes to speak of himself as a *person,* or an *I,* or a *self.*

The difficulty, of course, is found in the question: What do we mean when we speak of ourself as a *person?*

Any given answer to this question is mysterious and ambiguous, because we are referring to the grounding center of man's self-awareness. Man himself appears to be a thing; and we tend to speak of man as an embodied person or subject; but what *person* is never becomes self-evident. Man is aware of himself as being an embodied spirit, a transcending act present to himself. But how does one identify himself as *being* a person?

Some would say, as did David Hume in the eighteenth century, that there is no way by which we are able to identify the exact center of self-awareness. When we seem to enter inwardly into self, we come face to face with our perceptions. We never confront the *I.*

Obviously, if we confront the *I* in any manner whatsoever, we do so through the medium of our perceptions. Yet to say we experience only our perceptions seems too narrow an assertion. Our perceptions are united to and proceed from a center, a living form of conscious-awareness. I am aware of *myself*, in and through my body, in and through a reflecting experience.

I am not aware of myself as an object or thing, but as a dynamic centering of my being and all its acts. The living center, or the *I*, remains continuously present through the organic individuality of the body.

In such a context I am able to define a human person as a living form of reflecting, conscious, awareness. The dynamic factors, it would seem, should be emphasized; for I am constantly able to actualize myself in new ways in and through a living relationship with my body, in and through a living relationship with the world and with other persons. In and through such modes of actualization, a person is always creating or destroying himself. Looking at this dynamic side, we are aware that our person is a mysterious centering of live energy, lighting up reality in intuitive manifestations. We are able to say, as well, that man experiences meaning in and through the *self*.

The person principle in man constitutes the uniqueness of each and every human self. The person distinguishes one man from the crowd. Each person has his unique manner of thinking, his personal viewpoint, his particular value system, his personal manner of living. Further, each human person is burdened with necessities and freedoms. One must live with his body, in a particular world, with particular people, facing the mystery of his deepest self.

Fifth, man is a *community essence*. For man to exist as a person in this world, he must co-exist with other people. As an organic center of self-conscious awareness he is confronted daily by other self-conscious centers, similar in almost every way to himself. The co-existence with others is, in its deepest meaning, a practical necessity, yet a most difficult situation. For the most part, a human person can adjust more easily to things, for he is able to control them. Other human persons cannot, or should not be, controlled; while, at the same time they are less stable and predictable than things. We hear it said: For man to exist, he must co-exist. But at times we fail to perceive the practical necessity implied in such an affirmation. Often, in speaking of the human ideal of creating community, we fail to perceive the actual conflicting purposes which exist in every community of people, as each person seeks to be himself and to find meaning in his life.

Community itself is a sharing among persons, of an interaction of life and consciousness. It is through the integration or ordering of human activity and consciousness that a group of people hold together in a continuity of activity, rendering it both concrete and distinct. In such a frame of reference, we speak of a family, a school or university, a business corporation, a state, a religious community. As Peter Berger remarks, a community has no other being but that bestowed on it by human activity and consciousness.

But, obviously, a group of people come and stay together for the achievement of some determinate purpose or goal. The purpose, in turn, is always associated with some intelligibility or meaning. A man integrates his activity and consciousness with that of others to find himself and to create meaning in his life. The work is accomplished in and through living personal relationships, yet never fully accomplished.

The uniqueness of each individual person is the gift and burden which a man brings to community. Every community is, in this sense, a living encounter and dialogue of individual persons. As a consequence, every community is unique because of the persons and the specific personal relationships.

Ideally, going far beyond the actual situation of practical necessity, a community is established and ordered to give the individual person meaning to his life in a context of freedom.

In considering community from an integrated empirical and experienced perspective, we perceive the coherence and interaction of everything. We reason to an end purpose. "Man is not the center of the universe as once we thought in our simplicity, but something much more wonderful—the arrow pointing the way to the final unification of the world in terms of life."[9]

Sixth, what ultimately grounds the creative energy of everything in the universe is a mystery; yet at particular moments, sometimes suddenly and unexpectedly, man experiences within himself a living

---

[9] Teilhard de Chardin, *The Phenomenon of Man*, p. 223.

encounter with a *Holy Presence*. One experiences not a thing as such, but an actuating Power or Spirit. This is the empirical fact of man's religious experience which in the East is often associated with one's deepest self; but with Judaism, Christianity and Islam, is further identified as a personal Presence.

What religious experience implies most directly, is not that *man* infers that a personal Presence and energy grounds his being—though man can and does make such inferences—but rather, that *God* discloses his Presence in and through human experience. This is what theology calls the *revelation* of the transcendent Mystery within the immanent grounding of creation, man, or events. In this sense man comes to speak of God's gracious disclosure. Again, religious experience does not infer that man does not interact in the perception of the grounding Presence but rather places the emphasis elsewhere. God grounds and interacts in man's existence. What is further implied is that God, as the grounding Energy, discloses his Presence in all things, though in a hidden or contrary manner; the intelligibility or meaning found in the center of things and events, and in terms of that order.

We are also saying, as one may observe, that God as the Grounding Spirit discloses his Presence in mystery; and only in and through the mystery can he be found and recognized. What is inferred here is that no one is able to take anything as evidence that God does not exist; rather God is disclosing his creative Spirit in the thing as it is. Again, if God cannot be encountered in and through the mystery of what man is, he cannot be found. How can one find God in other things if God does not disclose his Presence within the experience of man? Man's life is an internal self-realization before it is fulfilled externally.

But does God really disclose himself through his creative power or Spirit within man? This is, of course, a crucial question which man places to himself throughout life. Each man must walk in the path of a creature and experience meaning in the mystery of creation. Some will say with Martin Buber that man's total experience discloses a personal Presence. One knows who speaks and calls. One experiences that in the call he is claimed and may

66

respond, but always with freedom. Others will declare that man's so-called awareness of a grounding Presence is nothing more than a psychic projection; and what one calls a living encounter with God is no more than a conversation with the various levels of the self.

Man in his mystery, as we can see, raises the problem of God. The problem of theology finds its center in the mystery of man as a unified embodied subject or self-conscious spirit. Does a divine disclosure—or an address through the medium of a word—occur within the inwardness of man's deepest spirit? Is man, in what he is, carried into a world beyond our visible world of appearances to a speechless thou-to-thou or spirit-to-spirit confrontation?

Theological anthropolgy in such a perspective directs man's attention to himself, his relationships with the world, and his life with other human persons. Each man must answer the question personally.

In my empirical self-awareness just who am I? What do I perceive? Just what is the meaning of my perceived intelligibility?

Theological anthropology cannot remove the mystery implied in the visible universe, in history, and in a man's person and life; yet it can and should indicate, out of a perspective of human self-awareness and the coherence of the whole of reality, that God as a creating Presence *appears* to interact with the whole of creation. He appears to be the grounding principle in everything, yet allowing things to be what they are; he appears as a dynamic Spirit to ground man's existence as an embodied spirit; he appears to be the Presence associated with his values and conscience; he appears to impress meaning or intelligibility into the minds of men; he appears to enter into intimate I-thou relations with men; he appears to direct —as a father in his own home—the direction of evolution and history.

If theology did not make such specific declarations, human life might remain confused and paradoxical to many; for certainly, if God does exist, someone should seek to respond to the intelligibility of the Lord's presence.

Man, from the perspective of theological anthropology, is a self-conscious embodied spirit. In his self-consciousness he is present to himself. Here, as one can perceive, man is defined as he experiences himself rather than as a particular thing. At the same time, and from an empirical self-awareness, man experiences a living relationship with a holy Presence. Such a religious experience is obviously situated. It is not always present to man; but it takes place at unique moments, usually when one is alone and solitary. At such moments, man's self-understanding of himself takes place on the level of consciousness. One experiences that he is addressed by a loving and creating Presence.

Religious experience, however, may not necessarily affect the level of consciousness openly and directly. It may, instead, be vague and affect, rather, the total man and his total manner of acting. This means that spirit—either man's spirit or God's Spirit—is not experienced at times, since one can perceive spirit only by conscious awareness. Man is thrown into the world of things and objects. Difficulties present themselves and, obviously, spirit is not a thing or an object. In such a general human situation, the more a man turns away from his personal awareness of a holy Presence, the more he turns from his personal awareness as being present to himself, the more he tends to be shocked and scandalized by the mystery of reality and his own human nature.

Today, when we look at the total action of man, we observe how his manner of thinking and living is situated towards finding meaning in this world rather than in God or in some world beyond death. We come to speak of secular man and the process of secularization. We say that modern man is keenly aware of his personal freedom and that he tends to think and act in a functional manner; he seeks to find meaning in his personal life and in living in this world. As he seeks to find meaning in this world, he avoids domination by religious authorities, institutions, ideas and values. In the process, society and institutions also become secularized. To some degree, at least, man's self-understanding is cut off from the sense of the holy and of a grounding Presence.

Yet, theological anthropology affirms that man in confronting himself confronts the grounding actuality of God. The question arises: How can this be?

1. One must say, in the first place, that the word *God* does not point to a thing or being as such, but rather, to a dynamic Act, Power, or Presence. God is a reality completely other than any object we know in this world. Furthermore, as our consciousness informs us, we do not confront God face to face, but only in and through the medium of our consciousness and a lived experience of the Holy. We seem to be lured by a loving Presence.

Our intellectual, human experience of the depths of our self does confront each man with a dilemma. Am I merely confronting my own life principle or spirit; or is my spirit grounded in an immanent yet transcendent Spirit?

Each person faces the dilemma in a condition of freedom and must answer on his own personal responsibility. In a real sense, one can only witness to the light that comes to him as he is situated in a particular time and place. Men are led to speak of God according to the particular and different features of their experience. One cannot blindly say, with dogmatic self righteousness: God exists! Rather, with some sense of personal freedom and responsibility, he must confess: My living experience of reality and myself discloses to me a holy Presence. Otherwise, in an experience of non-meaning, he may judge that he must proclaim with an opposite form of self-righteousness: God does not exist!

2. Again, we must observe that man's self-awareness is always associated with a particular time and place. Modern man's experience of reality, together with his specific consciousness, is directed towards a secular world and the people he confronts and lives with. One seeks to a large extent to be free of ideas coming out of the past and to be open, instead, to whatever new reality comes to him at each moment. Again, rather than seeking for the meaning of the

whole of reality, one seeks from moment to moment for the fulfillment of *life*.

However, we must notice the paradoxes found in man. To be
himself modern man seeks to be free, personally responsible, and to
celebrate life in and through love and friendship. He seeks, further,
to reject the evil and horror of the past. To be himself man must
ever seek after higher actualities and the new. Man discloses by
his total action that he is embodied spirit. In such a context he
searches for the meaning of life. In one way or another he comes
to the insistent question of Tolstoy: "What do men live by?" If
one comes to agree with the answer: "LOVE," then he comes to
the ultimate problem of man: Are we not grounded in Love? We
are able then to understand the general condition of man. The more
one tends to seek after the fullness of life and to celebrate its gifts
and joys, the more one must face the deepest truth of human
existence.

Chapter 4

Man as an Historical Reality

Human Experience Within Time and Place

As we have observed, the questions, What is man? and What is the meaning of human existence? are abstract and general. Such questions appear cut off from the life of a particular man as he must face the whole of reality in the context of his historical situation, as he must live in a particular time and place. From the concrete situation of a particular person, the questions are raised as one faces the real world. With tones of concern one asks: Who am I? What is the meaning of my existence?

Placed or thown into a particular world, these questions can be answered only by me through my intellectual awareness and understanding. I answer the questions out of the context of my particular human existence. What other persons perceive, say, or do, may aid me in my self-understanding; but the social process of human consciousness cannot dispense me as man from asking and answering the questions. Obviously, again, others will question and challenge my self-understanding, especially as I am joined to them in a particular institution or community. Yet, I am the person who must question and answer. Again, not only do I face a particular world and particular people, but I also face my particular religious experience; and I must answer the questions as a lonely human person.

I have at my disposal three modes of knowing: first, my empirical or scientific mode of knowing; second, my perception of the whole of reality; and third, my religious modes of knowing. These are the modes of knowing described by Max Scheler. Yet they were obvious to the ancients and indicated in the first article of the *Summa* written by Thomas Aquinas.

Following these three modes of knowing we can define man in general and abstractly, or concretely as a person enters into a living communion with what is known. Abstractly, and from an empirical manner of knowing, we can say that man is an embodied, living organism. From a philosophical viewpoint we can say that man is an embodied spirit open to the infinite or an embodied spirit in whom the intelligibility of reality is disclosed. From a theological or religious perspective we can say that man is an embodied spirit grounded in an immanent yet transcendent Presence. Concretely, the truth or meaning of such general statements are experienced by me in a personal and historical manner, from moment to moment, through my consciousness. I am present to myself as an embodied organism. I enter into living communion with myself as an embodied spirit through my consciousness and perceive from moment to moment the intelligibility of reality. It is I who must face, question and respond to the grounding Presence in all things and in me. Such a concrete mode of knowing means that each human person experiences through his consciousness what it is to be a man and the transcendence found within. In the perspective of personal self-awareness men share their experience and give common answers.

I experience, further, from moment to moment, my personal *human condition*. I am a *man*: good yet weak, inadequate to myself, forever failing in my responsibilities to God, to others, and to myself. I am, most truly, *a sinner*. My deeds disclose the truth, the failures of each of my days. I experience this condition to be with me, a centered selfishness, a closed narrowness. This condition is continually present and enduring. I speak of love and live in a kingdom of blindness and hate. I reject, constantly, the intelligibility and demands of reality. I reject others in their need. I am blind to or reject the ground of all I am. This condition I share with my fellow men. We live and stare at each other, waiting for the other to volunteer to do what we all wish but are unable to do.

Again, as a person living in the Christian community, I experience that I can proclaim in the name of my self and all other men what Paul the Apostle expressed out of his personal consciousness:

"We are justified by faith, we have peace with God through our Lord Jesus Christ. Through him we have obtained access to this grace in which we stand, and we rejoice in our hope of sharing the glory of God" (Rom. 5. 1-2). I remain what I am, a man caught up in all the complexities of the human condition. Yet, in living my life with God in and through the dead and risen Jesus, I experience a new consciousness. I live with hope, trusting that my life has meaning for me as a personal being. I am not a prisoner caught in the web of my particular past even as I pass from one tribulation to another. I am free for life and should remain free. I can live my life with love, joy, and at peace even as I survive at great cost to myself.

Such a shared Christian experience of life is not a way of living dictated by a decree of authority. It is a personal response given from moment to moment, objectified and socialized. It has the unchallenged authority of actual experience.

The Christian Reference to Objective History

Christian understanding of the meaning of human life is, then, not a simple subjective awareness or consciousness. It grounds the self-realization of human existence not only in the intelligibility of reality, but with specific historical events. This historical grounding of a man's self-understanding is also associated with an historical religious community: ancient and new Israel, an historical people of God.

Ancient Israel, as a community of people aided by a shared religious awareness and the open proclamation of its prophets, experienced a life of continual dialogue and communion with God through the medium of historical events. Such an historical understanding always referred back to one of two possible historical foundations. First, it was said, God called to Israel through Abraham. This tradition is represented in the story of Abraham given in the book of Genesis (Gen. 12. 1ff). Its prophetic confirmation is expressed in the accepted words of the community: "Look to Abraham your father and to Sarah who bore you; for when he was but one I called him, and I blessed him and made him many" (Is. 51.2). The second tradition referred back to the historical event of the Exodus out of Egypt. This was the moment in time when God redeemed his people from slavery and disclosed himself to be gracious, loving, and compassionate. "To maintain that the exodus from Egypt is a symbol only, that the essential point is the general idea of liberty which the story signifies is to disregard the heart of Jewish faith."[1]

These two historical traditions were united in a literary form through the story of the patriarch Joseph (Gen. 37-50).

History itself from the religious understanding of Israel receives its deepest meaning from the Spirit or dynamic holy Presence who creates. From such a viewpoint the intelligibility of creation can be represented in and through the image form of primeval history (Gen. 1-11). Such an historical, yet symbolical, story of creation does not contain any scientific material other than the empirical evidence of the visible universe as each human generation confronts and questions in a unique time. The story gives no scientific answers. Rather, it raises the human problem of intelligibility, the meaning of the world, the nature of good and evil, the meaning of human life and death, the purpose of man's creative and ruling powers, the values of human society and civilization. Such riddles are raised and answered out of a living relationship with God yet associated with the uniqueness of every moment and event.

Christianity, or new Israel, accepts the basic historical understanding of old Israel and is truly united to it in a shared religious understanding. The God of the Christian is the God of Abraham, Isaac, and Jacob. In this sense, the life of Abraham, Isaac, and Jacob is lived on in each human person and in the community. To a Christian, as to a Jew, God can and does disclose his Presence through creation, through a call addressed to each human person, through a uniqueness associated with particular historical events. Accepting the perspective that events in time can be unique, Christianity rests its past, present, and continued religious understanding on

---

[1] Abraham J. Heschel, *God in Search of Man*, New York: Harper and Row, 1966, p. 201.

specific historical events: the life, death, and resurrection of Jesus of Nazareth. From such a frame of reference, to say that the resurrection of Jesus is a myth symbol, rather than a unique event on the borders of time and place, disregards a basic Jewish understanding. From a human viewpoint, the temptation is to think and say that every moment of time, every event, is the same; whereas, the opposite is true. Every moment of time, every historical event, is unique.

From a human viewpoint, the temptation is to think and say that an embodied human existence after death is impossible. Every man must die and that is the end of his life. But from the Jewish religious understanding, the resurrection of Jesus is an event associated with time and is unique. As a consequence, a Christian understanding affirms: in and through the mediating activity of the risen Lord man is able to live a life on earth of genuine human freedom. One may question the truth of such statements of fact. In some real way every man does. We question the ruling authority and power of the dead and risen Jesus. The acts of divine manifestation, however, are not verified by human truth statements but by God's dynamic energy.

From a human standpoint, questions are always placed, because we confront an ineffable mystery. We are always asking, from moment to moment: How can I say that I have a true insight and understanding into the intelligibility of the visible universe, human existence, the order and purpose of history? How can I say that I have a true insight into the historical intelligibility of the Jewish exodus? How can I say that I have a true insight into the meaning of the person, life, death, and resurrection of Jesus of Nazareth?

With such questions we approach the depths of a man's personal faith. We seek to perceive and objectify what a person understands darkly. We seek to find expressed in human language a content that no man can declare.

The Problematic of Historical Awareness

Man's self-understanding of reality arises out of his awareness, consciousness, intuition at each present moment. In this perspective, man's evaluation of truth and error, beauty or ugliness, good and evil, are given in a living personal relationship with reality. As a consequence, man's understanding changes from moment to moment. At the same time, we know from our intellectual or philosophical manner of perceiving that man's self-understanding is always in the context of the whole. My living out of my conscious awareness, at each and every moment, belongs in such a context of coherence, yet in living association with the uniqueness of past historical events. The same situation holds for the common experience of a community of people. Who and what I am, how I live, how I perceive and understand, the pictures and symbols I use to express my understanding, take a coherent intelligibility as my present is lived in continuity with the uniqueness of past events, yet open to the happenings and events of my future.

But how do I perceive that present and past events are, truly, saving events? How do I come to have an historical or living understanding of the meaning of such human terms as grace, justification, redemption, salvation?

Obviously, the Jewish community has had and continues to have a living experience of a personal Mystery. Out of this grounding awareness Israel lives, thinks, looks at the world and life. At the same time, an Israel experiences life in and through the uniqueness of each historical event, it measures and objectifies meaning through a living confrontation with its sacred literature, the Bible.

The ancient Greeks, like each man, experienced the intelligibility associated with historical events and were aware of the problems associated with human history. One need only recall the writings of Herodotus (c. 484-425 B.C.) and Thucydides (c. 460-400 B.C.). Yet, the attention of the Greeks was directed towards expressed thought, objectified with terms associated with the cosmos (cosmology) and Being. The Greeks sought to capture truth, or the real, through their intuitions and to objectify it through the truth of judgments.

The ancient Hebrew and primitive Jewish Christians experienced the world of the moment and of time. Each lived with a preconceptual certainty associated with a consciousness of fidelity.

76

Such a lived certainty is truth (*emeth*). One is overwhelmed by the presence of a holy Mystery, and through concrete acts raises this awareness to the level of self-reflection and understanding. The nature of this constant, loving Presence may be questioned later. One in his lifetime may even come to ask the question, Does God exist? Man's subjective experience is not always the perfect test of the real. One must live out the meaning of reality in an historical context, through the coherent unity of his consciousness.

Such a lived experience of truth, or of God, is not timeless; rather to the contrary, it must be confronted time and time again. Further, God's faithfulness (*emeth*) must be made manifest, disclosed, or revealed again and again. One could experience a void rather than God; at times God appears to be silent, absent, dead.

The context is always one of free personal relationships. God's creating and loving Presence is made manifest as a personal constancy—from moment to moment, time and time again, in the past, in the present, in the future. In this perspective, Israel trusts God and expects God to be faithful, true, or constant in the future. Contingent and historical events are the basis of such an experience of human existence. The coherence of the whole is experienced in the present, remembering the past, and in an openness to the future. God on his part has the freedom, burden, and responsibility of disclosing his creating and gracious Presence in and through concrete manifestations associated with time.

How do I perceive that present and past events are saving events? The answer is: through this overwhelming Presence which brings me to self-understanding from moment to moment. How do I come to have an historical or living understanding of the meaning of such terms as grace, justification, redemption, salvation? The answer is that of Martin Buber: in and through my living relationships with the world, with others, and the holy, grounding Thou. At the same time we are aware of the tension of opposites or contraries. If any answers are truly given, they come to each of us as a light shining in darkness.

Yet, due to the influence of Greek philosophy, Christianity tended to stress conceptual knowledge and to represent what the human

77

mind knows in terms of things or beings. The human intelligence knows reality or truth in and through ideas or concepts. We notice this tendency, for example, in the Kantian critique of pure reason. Pre-conceptual factors associated with human awareness were not considered. It would have been difficult for Kant to understand how a human person could have a living experience of a Presence rather than of a thing.

A change, however, did occur in the late 18th century. An appreciation that God must meet man in the depths of his living consciousness became obvious with Hegel's *Phenomenology of Mind* and his *Philosophy of History*. William Dilthey (1833-1911) indicated in his *Critique of Historical Reason* how every human experience is an historical happening. Each human person comprehends meaning in an historical context through the coherent unity of his consciousness. Man is able to interpret past events and the intelligibility of history through the psychological structures of human existence.

Martin Heidegger in *Being and Time* changed the perspective. He no longer considered the historicity of man as a mere understanding of the intelligibility of past events but emphasized that man's existence is by its nature an historical consciousness, and man lives and acts with an historical understanding. This historical perspective of human existence is not only psychological, as it was with the viewpoint of Dilthey, but ontic. Each human person lives and acts at every moment through an historical understanding of the meaning of reality. Man lives within a temporal, historical understanding of being. Being discloses itself to each person in some historical context of meaning.

If man's awareness is open to the ground of all reality, yet associated with a specific historical understanding of meaning, then men can in some real way experience the creating and loving Presence of God in acts related to historical events. Further, within the same perspective, men can confront a basic meaning of human life as it is passed down through a living, or written, historical tradition.

Associated with man's historical understanding of meaning, which goes on from moment to moment, is his *social* awareness. Man in society lives in a particular world that is real to him, though each person perceives it in his own way; and he knows with some degree of conviction that this world possesses particular characteristics of truth and error, beauty and ugliness, good and evil. Usually he takes his world and knowledge for granted. He experiences it. What is real for the Russian is not real for the American. The personal and social experience is different. This knowledge is developed, maintained, and transmitted in a social situation. One says the same thing when he affirms: Man's consciousness is determined by his social being.

Again, there is some sort of real relationship between the expressed thought and an underlying awareness. I internalize my consciousness and express it in my own way: This is how it is with me. Further, I order my experience and meaning around the world of the *here* and *now*. I do this by my total action. I make my world. At times man may think that his life has no ultimate meaning; but to be a man in the world means to give ordered intelligibility to his thoughts and actions. Finally, I share my experienced meaning of human existence with others. I must, in some way, live in my own world. At the same time, I continually interact and communicate, or dialogue, with others. We organize a common world or society though in a form of tension. We share meaning and interaction even as the perspective of each person both changes and is different. Often, in such a social world I lose myself and become lost. Often, I both lose and find myself as I change my viewpoint and experience a new consciousness and a new way of life.

In an historical and social situation the truth or intelligibility of reality is experienced from moment to moment. The whole truth is never given; rather, each man joined to his fellow men lives each day on the truth he experiences out of an inherited social tradition and in a search and journey towards the future. From this perspective, the wholeness of truth lies before us in an unknown future. Men find and perceive the meaning of who they are and where they are going in the context of history and shared communal experience.

Each historical community has its own history of shared understanding associated with a religious awareness. "No human society from the most primitive to the most completely civilized, has ever existed without a religion of some kind. This can only signify that the source of religion must lie in some characteristic of human experience which is common and universal."[2] The understanding is internalized in religious experience, objectified in statements and human acts, hardened into institutions, taken for granted, and often not verified beyond the present awareness. The world of everyday life proclaims itself, though I have the capacity to doubt and to challenge its truthfulness.

What man experiences is his present which comes to him as an inheritance from the past. Present meaning or awareness must prove itself, however, in the future. And here we measure the future in terms of the present. The future of man from this standpoint has meaning in living relationship with present understanding. From the religious perspective, then, as I experience my life to be grounded in the Presence of God, in shared love, and personal freedom, I project this consciousness into the future. I trust, believe, hope, expect that I will share an eternal life with God. This transcendent experience in each man within his body receives a transcendental historical explanation. This allows the community to picture out, in terms of space and time, the final human destiny in an *Eschatology*.

When one lives out of the certainty of God's realness and loving closeness, one tends to trust his constancy, but from moment to moment, in the face of unanswered ultimate questions. Such perceived meaning is not purely subjective but is associated with the intelligibility of the real world. Yet, man's awareness is true only from a limited perspective. He cannot perceive the full and complete meaning in this life. The complete truth is not given to him. One responds to the certainty of God's realness by a living personal relationship extended to God in love and trust. Ultimately, God must prove his existence. Ultimately, God must prove his fidelity. Man can only trust the mysterious Presence in life and in death.

---

[2] John MacMurray, *Persons in Relation*, London: Faber, 1961, p. 156.

The common Christian understanding of man and the meaning of human existence, in the context of historical awareness, have been expressed in literary form through the Old and New Testaments. The New Testament will speak of the new way of Christian life in terms of *charis* (grace), *dikaiosis* (justification, vindication, acquital), and *soteria* (salvation, deliverance, preservation, redemption). From an historical perspective, these terms have a twofold meaning. They refer, first, to a personal and shared human experience; and, second, to the uniqueness of historical events.

1. Christianity, from the perspective of the New Testament writings, is a new way of life. "But Saul, still breathing threats and murder against the disciples of the Lord, went to the high priest and asked him for letters to the synagogues at Damascus, so that if he found any belonging to the Way, men or women, he might bring them bound to Jerusalem" (Acts 9. 1-2).

The good news, or the gospel, is the announcement of what God is doing in each and every person through the risen and acting mediator—Jesus, the Messiah, or Christ. The Christian way of life is a communal experience of God's saving act. We call our subjective or personal awareness of God: grace, justification, salvation. The Christian believes he is on the way to eternal life. Such a new manner of living, associated with man's consciousness, is not the pure product of human self-understanding but a response to God's Presence and call. Human thought, or self-understanding, is not faith.

From such a viewpoint, associated with his personal life, Paul the Apostle writes: "I am not ashamed of the good news: it is the power of God for salvation to every one who has faith, to the Jew first and also to the Greek. For in it the justice of God is revealed through faith for faith; as it is written: 'He who through faith is just shall live'" (Rom. 1. 16-17). This is the proclamation of apostolic preaching. God pours out his Spirit (dynamic Presence) in and through the risen Jesus (Acts 2. 17ff; Acts 4. 2). God is acting and reigning over men through Jesus Christ,

81

though in an historical context. "The time is fulfilled, and the kingdom of God is at hand: repent, and believe in the good news" (Mark 1. 14). "God so loved the world that he gave his only Son, that whoever believes in him should not perish but have eternal life. For God sent the Son into the world, not to condemn the world, but that the world might be saved through him" (John 3. 16ff).

From this horizon of understanding, the mystery of man is an historical manifestation of God's creating and loving care. The truth of man is not disclosed in and through statements, as such, though such statements may represent the truth of the mystery. Rather, the truth of man is disclosed through a life with God, which I experience as mediated through the risen and glorified Lord.

2. The good news of what God is doing in each and every man is mediated through historical events.

We may admit that a deep religious experience is remote from modern man. If he experiences the mystery of the Holy at all, it is more as a sense of emptiness, or a void, than as a personal Presence. In such a human situation it is difficult or almost impossible to think of the universe as a creation with its intelligibility centered in the life of each man as he lives from day to day. Daily events seem to have very little or no meaning. On the other hand, when we reflect for any length of time, we realize that each and every man does find some meaning in his life, and that the meaning is mediated through his daily actions and the events that happen or take place. Man's religious experience, likewise, comes to him through the world in which he lives. Man lives in an order of events. Intellectual and prophetic insights are events, as are moments of self-reflection, prayer, and decision. Free decisions, further, make man's history and help create the purpose we find in life.

In such a frame of reference, then, we are able to say that our personal awareness is mediated through historical and social factors. Men represent such an experience through pictures or symbols, referring to time and space yet transcending them. Within such a symbolic viewpoint, creation is God's first actualization of man's salvation; and this creative process includes the creative endeavors of man himself, who is created in God's image; and Christian experience proclaims that God's creating Presence actualizes itself in history through a gracious kindness and constancy. Israel speaks of God's covenant Presence among the people. The new Israel speaks of a new covenant, a new manner of experiencing God's loving Presence through the death and resurrection of Jesus, the Messiah.

What creation is, then, what man is, what human life means, what sin is, what salvation is, becomes disclosed in and through the events of history.

God's Creative Presence in Man's Experience of Salvation

God's *creative* power, or Spirit, acting in the universe, has its most perfect realization in the concrete life of each individual human person. This loving actualization of God's Presence in man the Bible calls *salvation*. What this symbol word indicates, or points to, is experienced in man.

The term salvation, or *jasha*, should be understood in a creative perspective. It denotes two elements: a deliverance from a distressing human condition or situation, and the fulfillment of a new condition of human life as a victory over evil. Such an actualization of God's creative power affected the community life of Israel. "Israel is saved by the Lord with everlasting salvation" (Is. 45.17). This dynamic actualization of God's creating presence is realized in the Christian community through the risen Jesus. "For in him all the fullness of God was pleased to dwell, and through him to reconcile to himself all things, whether on earth or in heaven, making peace by the blood of his cross" (Col. 1. 19-20). Not only is the risen Jesus the Mediator or Agent of a new creation, but he is also the final term of its actualization. In the man, Jesus, God's creative Word is fully declared and his plan for creation definitely accomplished.

What God offers to man is the *gift* of salvation. As an historical embodied thing, man is a created object. He need not be, he not always was, he need not continue to be. If he survives death, it will be because the life beyond death is also gift given. In some real, though mysterious manner, all that man is and does springs from an immanent creating ground. Man is a mystery given to the world but not comprehended. Men, rather, experience the gift of life rather than know its depths.

Beyond human life itself man experiences a need for the divine; he searches for a communion with the ground of his being as a personal Presence. We perceive this as we turn in on our deepest self. "As a hart longs for flowing streams, so my soul longs for you, O God. My soul thirsts for God, for the living God" (Ps. 42. 1-2). Such a companionship is also gift given. No man can force its fulfillment from his freedom. The Spirit of God, like the wind, comes and goes as it wills with its freedom. This coming to man on God's part is an act of instilling a new creation, a new creative moment of shared life in a man's history. Such a shared communion with God is experienced to be the gift of salvation, a gift of a new conscious life.

Such an historical experience of the truth of human nature is not expressed in the Bible by any ordered synthesis. Rather, what is indicated is man's awareness of a dynamic Presence which becomes the promise of an eternal inheritance. The Christian associates his experience of this communion with the risen Jesus. God "destined us in love to be his sons through Jesus Christ, according to the purpose of his will, to the praise of his glorious grace which he freely bestowed on us in the Beloved" (Eph. 1. 5-6). "We who first hoped in Christ have been destined and appointed to live for the praise of his glory" (Eph. 1. 12). The experience "is the guarantee of our inheritance until we acquire possession of it" (Eph. 1. 14). This experienced and shared life is grace. "For by grace you have been saved through faith, and this is not your own doing, it is the gift of God" (Eph. 2. 8ff). The experience is shared with others through the Eucharist (Luke 24. 30). In some way, the whole of creation waits with longing for the revealing of the sons of God (Rom. 8. 19). But such a statement is based on a life experience associated with hope rather than on empirical evidence (Rom. 8.

24-25). "Faith is the assurance of things hoped for, the conviction of things not seen" (Heb. 11. 1).

The Bible will, at times, picture out a final consummation in symbolic language placed within the framework of an ancient cosmology. Such a way of speaking is always the representation of an understanding associated with a particular historical period. Pictures from space and time are used to describe a life which transcends the conditions of time and place. What is basic is the specific religious experience and understanding.

The Limitations of Historical Experience

In some way, when we attempt to perceive the nature of man and his life, of myself and my existence, the knowledge and consciousness arise out of human experience. We perceive, further, that we intuit the truth or reality, but never the whole truth even though we are experiencing the wholeness of what it is to be a man. Our knowledge of man is limited and the content of truth is limited, though we do protest at times that we know the truth. This is our general, yet coherent, knowledge of man.

From my empirical mode of knowing, I am present to myself as an embodied organism. In this mode of knowing, though I may not be consciously aware of it, there is a living play of opposites: the energy of electrical quanta and waves and the active contribution of my mental experience. Not only is the sense data given by a transcending experience, but atomic particles do not enjoy self-awareness. Through sense data I perceive that I am an embodied organism. This is my intelligible perception. I perceive and experience that this is true. Yet such insight is limited. I do not know the whole truth.

From my intellectual mode of knowing, I enter into living communion with myself and perceive, from moment to moment, the intelligibility of reality. Further, I experience myself to be free. But how can this be? I do not know. All I have is my living experience of being a man.

From my religious mode of knowing, I experience at times that

I am grounded in an acting personal Presence. At some moments I respond with attention and love. At times I experience an emptiness, a void. Just who and what am I? In some real way, I can only tell the truth of what I experience.

Again, if we look closely at the biblical explanation of the meaning of human life, a question always remains. What is man? What is stated as a witness or evidence is always incomplete, expressed out of a limited human experience of some present moment in remembered relationship to the past. From the viewpoint of the Bible, the intelligibility of the whole truth about man and his destiny belongs to God in an unknown future. Man does not know because he confronts a mystery. The biblical viewpoint was limited further by a particular social and political experience understood within the framework of an ancient cosmology.

The perspective of the New Testament is unique in that it speaks about God and man in a living relationship to the dead and risen Jesus. Something new has happened and can be experienced. Yet even this new experience ends with a cry of trust: "Come, Lord Jesus!" (Rev. 22.20).

Man's limited experience of the truth implies that every generation must experience the problem of who and what man is in a particular world, which for us is a world of evolution and technology. God calls to each person as the creating ground of all he is, in his own age, with his particular human experience shared with others in community. What is experienced is a holy and loving Presence. The experience, affirmations, and images of such an I-Thou relationship are always limited. At some point they may actually become living forms of a Platonic evasion of life. Often we just picture things out. We avoid what is and should be.

Chapter 5

The Hebrew and Christian Conception of Man

The Problem of Objectifying Human Knowledge

Man is the only being we know of in the world of visible phenomena who has a self-conscious relationship to his embodied self. A man experiences the intelligibility of what it is to be a man. Man experiences meaning through his total action. At the same time, man represents, or expresses, his self-understanding through ideas or concepts, and then objectifies this expressed knowledge in affirmations and language statements. We are able to say that man both experiences and expresses intelligibility or truth. Obviously, man experiences what he is conscious of, though there may be some illusions about such a subjective awareness. Obviously, again, men can experience what it means to be a man in different ways. Men and women, for example, experience the human differently; and it would seem that we may say the same thing with regards to ancient and modern man, and Eastern and Western man. The differences may be very important and should be noted. Man also expresses his knowledge and objectifies it as he, a conscious subject, confronts the objective world of his body, the universe, and other persons. Such objective expressed knowledge, or truth, is always given in a living relationship of a human person to an object. Man, it would appear, must always express and objectify his knowledge. But here an added difficulty arises: To what extent is such expressed knowledge true?

The Hebrew man in antiquity placed the emphasis on *experiencing* what it means to be a man; while the man living in the Roman and Greek world sought to *express* and *objectify* truth.

We say the ancient Hebrew emphasized existence while the Roman and Greek mind stressed the specific essence of things. In this context we are able to notice differences in human self-understanding and also a Christian tendency to ground religious experience in an ontological or metaphysical frame of reference. Christianity, it would seem, tends to rationalize the truth of man.

I do not mean to imply that either tendency is wrong or an evil. Rather, I would stress that man's manner of knowing is very complex; and, as a consequence, one must notice the peculiarities, the contrasts, the limitations. I, myself, think that a man by nature —to be a man—must rationalize his religious experience and place it within the horizon of the intelligibility of the whole of reality. One may say that he lives by faith alone, but some hidden assumptions about reality are implied. At the same time, I perceive a weakness in man's attempts to express and objectify truth. Such truth is given in a living relationship with reality; and man does not perceive everything and cannot express it fully.

When we enter into the world of man's knowing, we are in the strange area of signs and symbols. Man knows through his sense perceptions even as he perceives the intelligibility of himself through a total action. He also conceptualizes his living awareness together with his sense knowledge. He creates and expresses his ideas. Further, man expresses his knowledge through written and spoken language. In some sense, human language is artificial and belongs to the world of symbols; yet, language is used to express and to point to intelligible reality. Man makes objective statements in a living relationship to reality. We come to say that objective statements are partially subjective and partially objective. We can say "Yes" to them up to some point; and then we say "No." Direct experience is infallible. You experience what you experience. But symbolism is very fallible; colored objects in themselves are not exactly as one sees them; mental disturbances affect both our ideas and consciousness itself. Marx, Freud, and Nietzsche speak of man's false consciousness. Freud maintains that dream and neurotic symptoms create illusionary ideas. Marx maintains that man creates his system of ideas and ideals out of an economic and political situation; and, as a result, there is often present a false consciousness. Nietzsche maintains that man creates false and defective ideas of value through the weakness of his will to power.

As a result, men became *suspicious* of the possible presence of false consciousness, illusionary ideas, and represented errors.

At the same time, man's manner of knowing is related to his historical situation. Man is an historical being and has an historical understanding of himself. He interprets meaning in a living relationship to his time and place. He conceptualizes and represents his language statements in images associated with space and time. Man experiences what he experiences, but there is always the possibility of his having a false consciousness.

We are able to say that concrete human life is caught up in a web of living relationships. When it comes to the experience of the real, its expression in concepts and sense perception and its objectification in human language, we may respond and answer in terms of meaning or, in a contrary way, with suspicion and scepticism. The second way questions and contests the objective content of ideas of the sacred and the intuitive use of the analogy of being to enter into the whole. We doubt when we become suspicious that things are not as they appear, or that we ourselves suffer from the illusions of our consciousness.

At the same time, we should notice that we doubt because we seek to free ourselves from our illusions. We seek to reinterpret reality in terms of meaning. Man, as man, thinks he can discover truth and objectify it in some limited form.

The question or problem of objectifying human knowledge refers most deeply to our religious experience and the response we call *faith*. There are many ways of being conscious of and expressing our religious experience. In the Hebrew and Christian perspective of understanding, Martin Buber speaks of two types of faith. I may either trust someone or acknowledge a thing to be true.

There are two, and in the end only two, types of faith. To be sure there are very many contents of faith, but we only know faith itself in two basic forms. Both can be understood from the simple data of our life: the one from the fact that I trust someone, without being able to offer sufficient reason for my trust in him; the other from the fact that, likewise without being able to give a sufficient reason, I acknowledge a thing to be true. In both cases my not being able to give a sufficient reason is not a matter of defectiveness in my ability to think, but of a real peculiarity in my relationship to the one whom I trust or to that which I acknowledge to be true.[1]

In religious faith, as Buber says, my entire being is engaged. The totality of my nature enters into the process. The living relationship of my faith is a relationship of my entire being and action. My total person is engaged in the whole function of thought. But, obviously, I am able to emphasize a specific aspect of the living relationship. In this sense I may place the emphasis on trust; or, I may seek to acknowledge and accept.

The living relationship of trust leads, naturally, to acknowledgement and acceptance. The acceptance of experienced truth leads to trust. In a living relationship of trust, however, Buber says, the existent contact is primary. The emphasis is on the living relationship, experience, consciousness. Acknowledgement and acceptance, on the other hand, indicate the aspect of response which demands expression with the added factors of reflection and intellectual insight.

In the first type of faith, Buber says, a man 'finds himself' in the living relationship of faith; in the other, one is 'converted' to it. The man who finds himself in the living relationship of faith is primarily a member of a community; the man who is converted to faith is, primarily, an individual; and a community arises out of the coming together of the converted individuals. In trust, the other person is experienced as being near; in acknowledging truth some distance is implied.

The first experience of faith, Buber thinks, was common in Israel, especially in its early periods; while the second, was common in the primitive Christian community, the New Israel, especially in Hellenic Jewish Christianity. In Israel, the individual person finds himself in a religious community; his faith is a living trust in the guiding Presence of the Lord. The trust arises and continues out

---

[1] Martin Buber, *Two Types of Faith*, London: Routledge and Kegan Paul, 1951, p. 7.

90

of a person's living relationship with the personal Mystery. In Christianity, one had to be converted to a new intelligibility: that God had, and was, disclosing himself in and through the dead and risen Jesus. One had to reflect, speculate, perhaps even to doubt at times, so as to interpret and avoid a false consciousness. In the context of Hellenic culture one had to reflect to acknowledge the truth.

In the perspective of Buber, we realize that man both exists and thinks; he exists and experiences; he exists and becomes conscious; he exists, reflects, doubts, and searches after the truth. In religious experience, man exists and thinks. The two aspects are part of a whole, though one may emphasize his living rather than his reflection.

At the same time, we are caught up in the problem of objectifying human knowledge. Men live and think differently; men live and believe differently. But do we know our religious experience better than our self-reflection upon it and our interpretation of intelligibility? Most certainly we experience what we experience; and, in this respect, we know our religious experience better than our self-reflections, expressions and objectifications of it. But unless we conceptualize our experience it remains vague, empty, and subject to false consciousness. Yet, having said this, men still live and think differently.

Israel, as a religious community, tends to posit itself and its religious experience and trusts in the holy Mystery. Christianity from its beginnings has followed a reflective manner of living and believing. It posits itself in acknowledging and accepting the truth. It doubts when it becomes suspicious of its consciousness. At times it says: Unless I see I cannot believe; at the same time it confesses: the Logos became flesh. It seeks to capture its total human experience in the mirror of its ideas, language, statements, and affirmations. The Jewish community, to the contrary, seeks to posit itself as it exists. It trusts in God's loving Presence.

Both Judaism and Christianity seek after the meaning of human existence and a fullness of life. Both center attention on human consciousness and on the same religious experience of a living personal Presence. Judaism, however, seems more concrete or historically oriented. It tends to think in terms of myth and symbols. Christianity, basically, shares the same faith understanding as Judaism. Each believes in the God of Abraham, Isaac, and Jacob. Yet, Christianity, as it developed, became more reflective. Looking at it within the horizon of Western civilization, it became oriented towards philosophy and science.

Jewish consciousness says: I am and I live in a world of mystery and symbol. Christian consciousness says: I think and I live in a world of intelligible reality. Answers to the antinomy are never given in ready-made solutions. Men work out answers from one generation to another. Symbols point towards reality and the holy Mystery; reflection points towards intelligibility and a failure of understanding. With man, his *I am* and *I think* are not separate things; rather, they are the two tasks which all men undertake as they journey through life. Each completes and corrects the other.

Man, through a dialectic of concrete reflection—I am and I think —works out the problematic of objective human knowledge. Answers, of course, may be rooted in God's grace.

We should notice, finally, that an idea is abstract when it has no living relationship to our experience. For some, then, to speak of man in terms of God or Jesus Christ may appear to be no more than projected abstract ideas, with no basis in reality or the world. This remains so, at times, even though one talks in language about historical facts and events.

The Hebrew Conception of Man

The Jewish idea of man comes to us through the historical reality of the community of Israel, the people of God, as it has manifested itself in history and through the vision of its prophets and its thinkers. In general, Jewish understanding of man rests on the objectified tradition of the Torah, the first five books of the Bible, accepted as the vision of its prophets and called at times the teaching of Moses. The Bible itself is a story about man in history, though understood in relation to a creating and loving Presence. The

Talmud, likewise, is a book about man, the record of how men struggled with the problem of man. In this perspective, Judaism is not a religion about God, but rather, a religion about God-and-man.[2]

In general, as I have said, Jewish thought begins with man's historical or concrete experience—though always in the context of community—rather than with abstract concepts. This experience points both to the problem of man and his wholeness. In one respect, man is a mystery. He constantly asks the question: What is Man? as he experiences the question he is asking. On the other side, man experiences an open wholeness. He shares in the finite and infinite. He is the center, lord, and glory of creation. He enters into a creative relationship with the world of things, with his fellow men, with a holy Presence. He experiences a call to life and to destiny. He experiences both good and evil. He knows he must die.

When we look at the *Torah*, we realize that the Hebrew mentality tends to interpret man in two ways: first, by man's *living relationship* to the world (or creation), to his fellow men, and to God as a holy Presence; second, by looking at the *dynamic energies* found in each man. The meaning, or lack of meaning, which a man finds in his life, is constituted by his active participation in the created world; how he acts and reacts with his fellow men; and his living relationship with God. These relationships indicate and disclose the living tensions found in each man. Man, at the same time, is a live body. He is good and free, yet experiences within himself the mystery of good and evil and possesses inclinations towards good and evil. From this second perspective, man is a divided subject. He must fight the evil inclination at work within himself: his *Yetzer Hara*. At the same time, he must struggle to order his good inclination, his *Yetzer Tov*, towards a living companionship with God, while obeying his will. The struggle may cripple and destroy

---

[2] Cf., Martin Buber. The Knowledge of Man, New York: Harper & Row, 1966: Abraham J. Heschel, *God in Search of Man*, New York: Harper & Row, 1966; Abraham J. Heschel, *Man is not Alone*, New York: Harper & Row, 1966; Franz Rosenzweig, *The Star of Redemption*, Boston: Beacon Press, 1972; Elie Wiesel, *Night*, New York: Avon, 1972; Arnold Wolf, *What is Man?*, New York: A B'Nai B'Rith Book, 1968.

him. The first interpretation moves among experienced meaning. The second interpretation moves among forces. One interpretation may not be disjoined from the other.

1. The first interpretation: lived meaning. The Jewish understanding of man as represented in the *Torah* and throughout the Old Testament is an interpretation of lived meaning, or human experience. As a result, no unified doctrine of man is ever set down; and viewpoints may differ as one experiences the meaning of what it is to be a man in a specific way. Such a viewpoint is less idealistic than that of the Babylonians and Egyptians where man is represented as divine and born of the gods.

Man, in his first relation to the world, is experienced to be a living thing, formed by God out of the dust of the earth (Gen. 2). Man does not spring or emanate from God; rather, man is a *created* thing (Gen. 1). Man as a creature is distinct from God, even though man is grounded in God's dynamic Presence.

To say that man is a creature living in the world suggests, on the one hand, his total dependence upon his Creator; and, on the other hand, his position of lordship and glory in the universe. Man is a creative subject like God. His task is to rule over all things (Ps. 8).

The Old Testament does not define man as a personal being, but its language statements indicate that man experiences himself to be personal, so that each man has a task of his own in the world and for it. In this sense, man has a real value as a person and not merely because he is a member of a community.

Man's life in this world is transitory. He passes away like a shadow. He must experience death and return to the dust from which he came (Gen. 3.19). The spirit, or breath (ruah), returns to God who gives it; so that life in this world is experienced to be a wondrous gift. Nowhere in the Old Testament does man speak of the immortality of the human soul. Man does not experience this. What he experiences is his life in this world. He can, therefore, hope or trust for a continuation of life in a new world, pictured out as an underworld, *Sheol.*

Secondly, man, to be a man, lives in a shared life with his fellow men. Man is created as male and female. God gives man the joy of sexual life and the blessing of children (Gen. 1. 27-28). The woman is the equal of man, his helpmate, partner, and complement. Man, to be a man, cannot live without her. Each sex is for the other. They are united together in a shared unity through the living relationship of love. This basic union, as with all other human relationships, is affected adversely by the acts and presence of sin. Further, in the life shared between a man and a woman, emotions indicate meaning. Lived meaning experiences harmony, peace, joy, and love among men.

Lived meaning in Judaism, especially in antiquity, is basically human rather than religious. When one looks at the position of women in Jewish society, we notice how this group of people followed an Eastern manner of living. This held true for relations between friends, strangers and enemies, life as it was lived in a family, in community, in the relationships between the people and its rulers. For the most part, however, the human experience is always related to the living experience of God. Out of this viewpoint came high human modes of acting towards the weak, poor, widows, slaves, and strangers. When one experienced slavery, as the community did in Egypt, one experienced the human need for freedom.

In antiquity, Judaism shared a community consciousness. The community had an experience of meaning. Only in and with one's fellow men does man come to the fullness of life. Hatred, hostility, and injustice destroy both the meaning of life and human companionship. Human meaning and community are sustained by the positive efforts of open human affection. Human meaning was, then, a task which one struggled for in community with his fellow men, through trust, friendship, and justice. Such positive efforts subordinate and control the negative forces of fear, anger, and hostility.

Third, man comes to be himself through his living relationships with his world, with others, and, finally, with God.

Man is called into being through God's creative Presence and is a child, or son, of God. To be truly a man is to enter into living relationship with the holy Mystery. Man may, and does, sin; but the fundamental relationship remains because of God's creative Presence and will. Man is created to be a companion of God. Such a viewpoint arises out of man's experience. In this sense God is known as the personal Presence who concerns himself with the world, with history, and has a communion with each man.

Man can address God personally and immediately as "My God" and perceive that he is in a living communion with the holy Presence. One has immediate access to the King of Kings. He need not depend on ritual religious ceremony. In this perspective, when the prophets of Israel speak of knowing God, they are referring to a living communion with God rather than an objective conception. The experience is one of close union, and the meaning is clarified as the prophet looks at his world and its historical situation.

Man's living relationships of meaning are experienced most deeply when one is solitary, confronting the depths of his life.

Out of the depths I cry to You, O God!
Lord, hear my voice!
Let your ears be attentive
to the voice of my supplications! (Ps. 130.1-2)

2. *The second interpretation: the dynamic energies in man.* While the Hebrew interprets man from the evidence of human existence, he at the same time follows a second road: the experience of his dynamism. This is a manifestation springing from his inclinations and transcendental tendencies. Man struggles throughout his life to harmonize these energies with his experience of meaning.

From this dynamic viewpoint, man is a living, knowing being, a dynamic unity (Gen. 2.). Like God, he is a creative subject, the lord of the world, yet at times a slave and servant. Like God, he is able to place things in the light; yet his light is always associated with darkness. Like God, he experiences the meaning of good and evil. He senses the drama of human existence and history. One must live and act in a situation of power. He must labor to say yes or no.

To be man, the human person seeks after truth and wisdom; and one finds that "wisdom excels folly as light excels darkness" (Ec.

2.13). Yet, "that which is, is far off, and deep, very deep; who can find it?" (Ec. 7. 24). Man in seeking after truth lives out a contrasting act: one faces the real, but its principle is mysterious. Reality is both near and far away; and man acts out a double movement: he enters into a living relation with the near and distant. With him, a world exists; but, at the same time, a power within him soars beyond the given and his horizon of knowing. As Martin Buber writes: "No matter where you meet man on his way, he always holds over against himself to some degree, in some way, that which he does not know as well as that which he knows, bound together in one world. . ."[3] Man, with his energies, has a daily task: to seek after truth. What he finds in life is meaning, but never the ultimate meaning. "I have seen the business that God has given to the sons of men to be busy with. He has made everything beautiful in its time; also he has put eternity into man's mind, yet so that he cannot find out what God has done from the beginning to the end" (Ec. 3. 10-11).

But what is man to do as he faces the unknown? He must respond with his whole person with a transcendent openness. The life of man is to proceed from the known to the unknown, from the finite to the infinite, from the order to the mystery. Man's creative thinking drives him onward. He turns to the mystery and enters into living relationship with it, which at times he experiences to be personal. He comes to his response of faith. In this sense, faith is a living response to mystery but experienced in a relationship of meaning, love, and hope. In such a response is found the greatness of man. He is able to live by faith and through his free act to sense a Presence. He enters into a relationship of ultimate meaning.

Because the mystery remains, God is a continual question and concern to man. He may turn away and not be open to the mystery. At that moment, everything becomes absurd. What is engaged, then, in such human moments of temptation and sin, is the faithfulness of God. This is the truth of God's factual existence and the constancy of his call to a man in his weakness and darkness. "How long, O Lord? Will you hide yourself for ever" (Ps. 89.46)?

---

[3] Martin Buber, *The Knowledge of Man*, p. 62.

97

As long as man questions he appears to be open. He questions all his life. This is both his misery and his glory.

But since man is a living being, he must respond. How does he do so? Man must take a leap of action rather than of thought. This action must be compatible with man's essence as a living image of God. In such a context, religious truth is experienced in a living dynamism. Man, as a living, creative subject, encounters in his life the ineffable mystery of God. "In the religious life of Judaism," as Buber writes, "primary importance is not given to dogma, but to the remembrance and the expectation of a concrete situation: the encounter of God and men."[4]

From the Jewish viewpoint, man encounters the Presence of God in living out the events and deeds of his life. The heathen, then, is one who does not or will not perceive God's Presence and manifestations. Yet, man acts in many ways and in the face of the contradictions of life. He acts at times with an undirected urge of passion and blind emotion. His dynamism becomes evil as it destroys. It becomes good as it is directed towards meaning, justice, and love. "I have set before you life and death, blessing and curse; therefore choose life, that you and your descendants may live, loving the Lord your God, obeying his voice, and cleaving to him; for that means life to you and length of days. . ." (Deut. 30.19-20).

In this sense, the creating and loving dynamism of God is good; creation is good; evil, or what man calls evil, arises out of undirected and blind power, either from the blind energy of matter itself, or from the undirected and blind inclinations of man. Man as man, then, is basically able to both experience and choose good or evil. The full content of what this means is given in man's everyday life.

The 'Fall' did not happen once and for all and become an inevitable fate, but it continually happens here and now in all its reality. In spite of all past history, in spite of all his inheritance, every man stands in the naked situation of Adam: to each the decision is given. It is true that this does not imply that further events are deducible from the decision; it only implies that the human being's choice is that side of reality which concerns him as one called upon to act.[5]

---

[4] Martin Buber, *Israel and the World*, New York: Schocken, 1963, p. 14.
[5] Ibid., p. 17.

Man, then, in his daily life, experiences the contradictions which come from the presence of good and evil. The energy or power in creation and in man is good, created by God for his service and the furtherance of his creative work. Power becomes evil when it is misdirected. In the contradictions of life, man must experience its tragedies. In such a situation, redemption is not a deliverance from the presence of evil but a turning of the powers in creation towards the service of God. Human ethics in such a situation is related to man's living relationship to God. It is man's creative task to take the manifold energies inherent in creation and direct them towards meaning, justice, and love. Creation calls to the wholeness of things. God the Creator wills to give intelligibility to the whole of creation. Man is a partner with God in this creative effort.

What is the truth about man? From the Hebrew viewpoint man cannot possess truth as a thing. We cannot pick it up and put it in our pocket. Rather, one must serve truth by translating his energies into the creative relationships of his daily life. Truth, in this sense, is found only in human action. Men live out—or do—the truth.

The Christian Conception of Man

Christianity had its origins in Israel and on the level of concrete human experience. Only gradually, as the new Israel broke from the older community, and as it moved into the Hellenic world, did it become conscious of its own thoughts and manner of living and related these to the problems of what it means to exist. One then sought to perceive through the meaning of expressed ideas or concepts the specific nature of things and of man. We speak of this as the tension between the Christian religion and ontology.

In such a general frame of reference we are able to say that the understanding of man as found in the New Testament writings is the same as that found in the Old Testament.

Man experiences himself to be a living thing, a dynamic unit. He is good, though finite, a creature of God. No part of man is evil. Paul, the Apostle, considered himself to be a good man before his conversion to Christianity; and he considered himself a good man afterwards. Though man is good, he is weak.

99

To say that man is a creature is to perceive that he is caught up in a web of relationships. Man is man in his living relationship to the world, to his fellow men, and to God. Man becomes evil when the inclinations within himself become misdirected as to the world, one's fellow men, and God.

The world, or creation, is good. Man does justice to the world when he acknowledges it to be creation. Sin is a misuse of this good world, making an idol of it. When a man misdirects his living relationship to the world, he is in revolt against his nature. He alienates his deepest self. When a man confuses the world and God, he allows the world to become a power which dominates him, whereas it should not. Such a human lossness in the world can be expressed in mythological terms. Man surrenders to demonic powers; whereas, to be a man one should be free of such forces, ordering his concrete existence towards God.

But in what direction is a man to turn as he lives in his world? The answer of the New Testament is that man is to turn his whole person (*metanoia*) towards a living relationship with God as God's dynamic power or Spirit breaks in on him. One must stand firm in this fundamental relationship of human life. One must build on a rock rather than on sand. The stability of the human person with the needed peace arises out of this fundamental living relationship of the human person to the Power which is his creating ground.

Such a turning towards God has its realization in the totality of life. If one turns towards God, God turns towards him. Blessed are they, then, who know their need of God. Blessed are they who hunger and thirst to see right prevail. Blessed are they who suffer persecution for the cause of right. Blessed are the peacemakers. Man must set no limits to his goodness, as God's expressed goodness knows no bounds (Matt. 5. 48). Yet, a person can only act according to his nature and ability, with all his power. A person can will to be good with all his love; but each day he must experience in a new way how and whom he is able to love. Man follows the way of humanity and must begin again and again. Everyone sins, but everyone may turn back to the way towards God.

In such a perspective, the call of Jesus was to sinners. Those who follow Jesus accomplish this turning. Flesh is flesh; but spirit is spirit. God is always present and his Spirit is strong enough to enable the sinner to turn. "Ask, and you will receive; seek, and you will find; knock, and the door will be opened. For everyone who asks receives, and he who seeks finds, and to him who knocks, the door will be opened" (Matt. 7. 7-8). Immediacy to God is a living relationship established in the creation of every man. Man may turn away in a wrong direction, but the relationship remains. In this sense, he who turns towards God prays and delivers himself into God's Presence.

Man's perceiving and being, however, changed in a radical way with the death and resurrection of Jesus. The resurrection was accepted to be an event on evidence (cf., 1 Cor. 15.1ff) and experience. One experienced Jesus to be alive and in God. One has peace with God through this risen Lord. "Through him we have obtained access to this grace in which we stand, and we rejoice in our hope of sharing the glory of God" (Rom. 5. 2). In this horizon of understanding the risen Jesus mediates God's act and gives man a new experience of God's Presence. Such a new consciousness gives a new joy to life and a confidence or trust in a personal embodied life with God beyond death. This was a change in subjectivity affected by actual historical facts associated with the person and life of Jesus. It created a new situation: the primitive Christian community.

At the same time man is confronting the inner dynamism of his own mind and must encounter non-Christian philosophies. The sharper the apparent contradictions, the more urgent is the need to conceptualize in new modes of thought. To be a man means to question and also to seek the truth. Human experience is not to be restricted to one's consciousness or his religious experience. Man experiences the intelligibility of concrete facts and of himself as a living organism. Man also, as the Greeks well know, perceives the intelligibility of the whole of reality and analyzes, through his consciousness, individual entities within a framework of general coherence.

In the first ages of civilization, man, proceeding by the way of concrete thinking, endeavored to picture the whole of reality to himself in mythical symbols associated with a cosmology. The great prophets of Israel living in the 8th century B.C. had a more reflective consciousness and spoke, as did Jesus, of the immediacy of God's presence, considering the concrete events of political history. With Christianity, man has become more self-reflective. He is reflecting in terms of empirical fact, through explicit intellectual insight, and through a reflective religious consciousness, while placing the whole of reality within a framework of history.[6]

Once man begins to reflect openly on the unified wholeness of himself and the coherence of reality, his attention focuses on the static and dynamic aspects of reality. One endeavors to perceive the essence of things in the context of movement. From a static perspective, man appears to be an essence in movement: a unit of matter and spirit. As man appears to possess a specific nature, he lives under a law or order of grace. Again, while electrons and protons tend to remain electrons and protons, they are caught up in a dynamism of evolution. In this perspective, while man tends to remain in essence man, he likewise is caught up in the dynamism of the evolutionary process.

The static and dynamic aspects of reality, then, lead to the study of man under the headings of: matter and spirit; nature and grace; organism and evolution.

---

[6] Cf., Karl Jaspers, *The Origin and Goal of History*, New Haven, Conn: Yale Press, 1959, p. 1-21.

Chapter 6

Man as a Unit of Matter and Spirit

Duality in Unity

From an empirical mode of knowing, we may define man as a living organism. Organism in this sense means that man is a unit of well coordinated parts or organs which are instruments to purposes inherent in the whole. As a living unit he is an energized whole, a living body. Beyond our empirical manner of knowing, we perceive by a strange intellectual self-awareness that man is a living organized whole and that he realizes or achieves purpose through the parts of his body. It is, of course, a fact to be wondered at that man is a living organism. But what truly astounds one is that man, in actualizing his energy within himself, becomes a bearer of a unifying, transcending power or spirit.

Out of our self-awareness, then, we speak of man as embodied spirit with a duality in unity. The language comes out of man's reflecting consciousness and his personal involvement in being a man. The language points to an objective real world. We speak of such words as pointing signs or symbols; and man intuits that he is saying something true when he declares that he is an embodied self-presence and that the life principle in himself is a dynamic act or process.

Some people say that empirical evidence is the sole and only valid manner of studying man. Empirical facts about man are to be observed and recorded; nothing more. Men do, of course, follow such a method of procedure in biology, as man is described as a living organism. But, factually, the self-consciousness of man and his intellectual understanding is always associated with his empirical mode of knowing. Without such an intellectual perception there could be no biology. As a result, most men concede that when one studies man, an empirical and intellectual mode of knowing must unite in a synthesis. "Of course, mankind has been engaged on this job for some thousands of years, with some lack of comprehension of its full import. It is the business of philosophy to elicit this consciousness; and then, to coordinate the results of all such specialist enquiries."[1] Any idea or conception of an objective fact is the triumph of intellectual perception.

When we speak of man, however, we should make some real effort to distinguish our empirical mode of knowing from our intellectual insights. In man's empirical mode of knowing, mental insights interpret the impressions of our senses; but empirical knowledge is not the same as our insights of reflective self-consciousness. One should endeavor at some point to synthesize both manners of knowing. Yet, each in its kind is a specific and different way of knowing. Empirical human knowledge is always the starting point. Self-conscious reflection is the search for a solution of intelligibility.

1. *Man's empirical knowledge of himself.* When we look at man from the path through our senses, we notice specific details: He is a part of nature, a live organism, an embodied mind, with interactions between the energy of matter, life processes and mentality. In such a general frame of reference, we may say that man is a duality in unity; but as soon as we observe and analyze the details, we qualify the first statement by saying that man is a complex living unity.

Man as a thing belongs to the world of nature. By nature we mean that physical portion of reality which is known to man through his senses. From this viewpoint, man is a unity of bits of matter

---

[1] Alfred Whitehead, *Modes of Thought*, New York: Macmillan, 1968, p. 22.

Many of the problems about *definitions* considered in this chapter may seem, at first thought, irrelevant to modern human life and what we do with our life in society. Yet the issues about defining man's nature in terms of matter and spirit are the most crucial problems facing man today. One would soon appreciate the problem of making judgments about man's nature if he would read the work of Georgi Plekhanov, *Fundamental Problems of Marxism*, Moscow: Progress Publishers, 1974, and the work of V. I. Lenin, *Materialism and Empirio-criticism*, Moscow: Progress Publishers, 1973. These two books are considered classics in Soviet Russia and are to be found in every book-store in Moscow and Leningrad.

taken into the system as food and cast off in forms of waste. The matter may come to rest, or be in movement as chemical units or electrical energy. Each particle of matter has its unique qualifications. Some resist change; others appear momentarily as charges of radiation and disappear.

Scientific analysis of the patterns of physical-chemical phenomena found in man's body, down to the chainlike molecules of DNA, have led some biologists to follow a *Mechanistic* interpretation of man. In such a frame of reference, and following the viewpoint of LaMettrie, d'Holbach, and Helvetius, there is no basis for ascribing a soul to man. Man is a machine made up of bits of acting and reacting matter. Everything in man can be reduced down to the phenomena of chemistry, physics, and mathematics.

Such mechanism follows a reductionist path of thought. From this viewpoint, empirical evidence leads one to conclude that particles of matter make up the whole of man and of the universe.

The problem is: Has the Mechanistic position taken the part for the whole? No matter how one would answer this question, the following affirmation seems true: Man is embodied energy.

Vitalism, observing the presence of a vital force in man, speaks of man as a living organism. It affirms: If one follows either the path of development of a single man or the historical and evolutionary development of mankind as a species, some leap of quality in activity is always incarnated which surpasses a purely chemical pattern. Man, most certainly, is made up of atoms and molecules; but, at the same time, he is a living organism and a resultant descendant of some lower form of primordial life.

The difficulty, as one can see, centers on the symbol term: *living*. What is one saying when he affirms that man is a *living* organism? The body and brain of man are, obviously, a material system; but what is one saying when he declares that his body, or brain, is alive? Is there a unique material quantum present in living things, or a higher act or process of existing? No matter how we answer in and through our ideas, a real fact is happening. Man is a *living organism*.

To a large extent, man is content to say that he is a living body and lets the situation rest with the fact. If asked to specify what he means, he simply refers to the on-going processes of nature and describes meaning in physical or chemical terms. One simply says that being alive is an *epiphenomenon*, adding no further explanation.

But what does one mean by life? Traditionally, in the Western world one has answered the question by saying that life is the power or the capacity for immanent and self-perfecting activity. Some have answered in a more general way by saying that life is self-movement. I, myself, would say that life is a unified act of self-possession and self-movement. Life refers to the unifying act of a particular being. It is immanent to the being or possessed by it. It is an activity of a center giving a preserving movement to the being. When the activity no longer preserves the whole as an acting unit, one says that a particular kind of being has died or is dead.

When man dies, individual cells and organs in the body may still be alive; but a unifying act preserving a unified self-movement has vanished.

The difficulty is the fact that a unified self-movement is found in some manner in every particular being in the universe. The created universe is a unified dynamic field of acting and reacting energy. Men have come to observe and recognize this in the atomic age. As a dynamic unity of energy, every unit of reality may be said to be alive. Every particular thing in our dynamic universe, in its own particular way, tends to act as a unit, with a particular self-movement and self-possession. An atom, insofar as it is a unit, possesses its self-movement. We speak at times of live atoms, live coals, live wires, live bombs. Each unit of reality, then, may be said to be alive in its own particular way insofar as it is a dynamic unit of energy.

As a result of what man has come to know of the dynamic reality of the universe, and of the dynamic unity in each particular thing, we must say that there is no *absolute* opposition between so-called living and non-living things, between inorganic and organic things. When we stress the acting and re-acting energy shared among all things on the universe, and the dynamic unity found in each thing, we perceive, instead, the lower and higher forms of self-movement and observe the creative advance of things. There is some real continuity between a stone and a tree, for each shares in the acting and re-acting energy of the universe; yet, at the same time, there is a real difference. The tree possesses a much higher unified act of self-possession and self-movement. Further, it is extremely difficult to specify at times the unified act of so-called non-living things. We wonder whether atoms are actually what scientists say they are.

The difference in lower and higher forms of unified acts appear to be in the united act of the whole. We refer to this as its unitary life principle. In such a context, men have come to speak of *souls*. It is relatively easy to observe that there are live cells in a tree; often we fail to notice the unified act of life in the whole tree. It is easy to observe that an animal possesses a live organ, like a heart or lungs; often we fail to notice the unified act of life in the whole animal. Likewise, it is easy to observe the body unity in each man, or the life found in particular parts of the body, yet fail to notice that the life process in man is a unified act.

When we observe, further, the unified act of a whole, we notice the creative activity found in each living thing or, if one wishes, in each dynamic unit. The unified act of a thing takes the potentialities at hand and raises them to a new level of unified act. It is in such a frame of reference that we are able to speak of the creative advance in the universe. In each creative advance there comes into being a new unified act of self-possession and self-movement. We are able to observe new unified acts or things, a new possession of aim or purpose, a unique creative activity. Other potentialities are excluded. Further, the unified act allows for continuity out of the past, into the present, and towards the future.

It is in reference to the creative advance found in man that we are able to speak of him, as we observe him acting, as an organic unit of body and mind. The acting unity is the fundamental fact, though some, following Descartes, speak in terms of a separation of mind and body. There is one center of activity located in the brain, which claims the body as an organic unit and the total experience. There is one continuous act of body and mind, even though molecules of matter may come and go; even though there appear to be total lapses of consciousness in sleep.

At times we say, with a basis in observation, that man sees with his eyes. What we are saying is, as we observe with closer attention, the whole man as an organic unit sees through the organ of the eyes. The same fact holds for all of man's senses. Specific organs play a primary role in specific acts, but man acts in and through a dynamic unity. In the same way, man both observes and perceives that he knows, loves, wills, remembers through his brain; yet the whole man knows, wills, and remembers through a total action. There is an immanent, coherent, inter-relation of the whole and its parts.

To say, *I am*, stresses the total dynamic unity of man. To say, *I am in possession* of my sight, or knowledge, stresses the creative activity found in man. To say, *I am an organic unity*, stresses the inter-related activity and causation found in man.

If what we have said is true, then empirical knowledge reduces the whole of created nature down to energy or activity; but always materialized in dynamic units. The whole of reality appears to be a dynamic relation of interaction.

But what is the basis of all the activity or energy?

2. *Man's intellectual awareness of himself.* From an empirical mode of knowing we come to speak of man as a living organism, an energized whole, a living unit, a living body. But, beyond our empirical mode of knowing, though in a living coherence with it, we experience a strange intellectual self-awareness. Out of such a reflective self-consciousness, perceiving the openness found in man, we tend to speak of him as an embodied spirit, or as a unity of matter and spirit. In the immanent inter-action of living an embodied unity, man experiences transcendence. It is out of such experiences of self-reflection that one comes to speak of himself as an organic unit with *a living act* unifying the whole, yet trans-

cending the energy of matter. The unifying act, or spirit, is experienced to be more than matter.

When we look at a dead man, we perceive there is some difference between being dead and alive. When a man is alive, there is present a unified act pervading the whole and each of its organized units. The whole life process of man is one of interaction between the parts and the whole to create unity, allow it to develop in the presence of opposing tensions, and to maintain it. The basic difficulty of transplants is to incorporate and perfect a life process found in one organ with a shared activity possessed by the whole, physically, chemically, electrically, and in communication with a center found in the brain. Then one will immediately add: there must be some live communication with the mind or psyche. This unifying activity of mind is the most baffling occurrence of nature. The hidden depths of the unifying act, or soul, of the body we both point and refer to when we speak of the *subconscious*.

Out of our living experience of being an embodied spirit we come to say three things: first, "*I am*" or "*I am a person*"; second, "I possess a *mind*"; and third, "I possess a *soul*."

a) *I am.* For a man to experience and affirm *I am*, the *I am* refers to his being in its totality, with a self-conscious awareness, embodied and living in a particular world. A unifying act of self-awareness has its own self as an object. An I is reflecting on its own I. The self knows itself as an *ego*, as a single acting individual with an experienced self-awareness. One experiences himself not to be a mere thing in this world but a *person*. One, however, does not merely experience but affirms. In this last sense, to say *I am* is a self-affirmation.

To be a person, a man does not need to express an open self-affirmation. But if and when he does, three aspects or modes become manifest: a knowing aspect (*Cogito*), an affective aspect (*Volo*), an engagement in the act of existing (*Sum*).

A person is a particular kind of a being with an ontological unity and autonomy. But in real life the personal autonomy is extremely relative. From moment to moment, from situation to situation, one must affirm what it means to be a person in his world.

Living in his own world, a person affirms his self-identity through his thoughts. He declares with Descartes: "I think, therefore I am." Through his expressed thought man comes to perceive that he is a person. This is a person's knowing and known relation. The person is recognized as self. Through his expressed thoughts man comes to recognize reality. This is a person's subject and object relation. Within such a perspective, each human person lives out the adventure of his ideas; and we are able to understand why Alfred Whitehead would say that man gropes his way towards civilization through his ideas, and why the adventure of ideas may be taken as a synonym for the history of the human race.[2]

Man, however, as a person is not a pure thinking subject. To be a person living in the situation of a real world, he must affirm: *I will.* From moment to moment, from situation to situation, a human person must consent to himself and to reality. At the same time, since man is not pure knowing subject but embodied, an emotional tone or quality is always present. But here the question arises: what does man seem to want as a human person? The answer to this question, out of the structures of human experience, seems to be: man, as a person, desires the *joy of life.*

Philosophers who have speculated on the meaning of life and on the destiny of man have failed to take sufficient notice of an indication which nature itself has given us. Nature warns us by a clear sign that our destination is attained. That sign is joy. I mean joy, not pleasure. Pleasure is only a contrivance devised by nature to obtain for the creature the preservation of its life, it does not indicate the direction in which life is thrusting. But joy always announces that life has succeeded, gained ground, conquered.[3]

Yet, a human person in consenting to his self and to reality, never finds himself or the joy he desires. Joy is experienced with the emotions of unrest. At the same time, value is experienced by a person in a living relationship with reality. At one moment a human person says "Yes" to his values; at another moment, he

---

[2] Alfred North Whitehead, *Adventures of Ideas*, New York: Macmillan, 1967, p. 3.
[3] Henry Bergson, *Mind-Energy*, New York: Macmillan, 1920, p. 23.

experiences himself saying "No." In consenting to life, as Heidegger remarks, man becomes concerned about what he is and what he desires. What he wants is never identified with what he is or experiences. Rather, he senses the emotion of estrangement and alienation. He cannot stand still. He must go forward.

To be a person is an engagement in the *act of existing (sum)*. *I am*; and I exist as an *I*. Man is grounded in an act of existing. As such an act man is a person, engaged in life, confronting reality, in a situation of limited freedom. Man is a living embodied person. In being this he is not identified with any other reality. He is not the *All*; only a limited, though creative, act of existing, deeply concerned about his person and his life. Heidegger expresses this aspect of being a man by saying that man has a living relationship to the act of existing which is, at the same time, a personal manner of understanding the intelligibility of reality. In living relationship to his person as an act of existing, a man knows, loves, and engages in action.

In existing as a person, man is free. He is free to be what he wants to be, though within limited circumstances. We say he is free in his world. He possesses a distinct creative activity. He can be master of himself and of some situations. He can make things happen. He can become what he is not yet. Sartre declares that man is condemned to freedom. To be a person means to be creative, free, and active. A man must labor at this task if he wishes to be and remain a person rather than a machine or robot.

In such a perspective we are able to understand the *ethical* tasks of man. Man is free to be a person, or said another way, man has the task or obligation to be a person. He cannot, or should not, hurt his person. He should not hurt the person of others. Rather, the triumph of human life consists in the creation of one's self as a free person and in aiding other human persons to find themselves. In this sense, to be free is to be ethical.

Again, from the viewpoint of man's creative activity in being a person, the essential tasks of human life must find their fulfillment in *society*. A community of persons—even when we consider the misdirections and failures—benefits from the creative activity

111

of all the members and renders the life of each person easier and more enjoyable. It is true, as Bergson remarked, that individual persons and society too often move around in circles instead of moving straight forward towards a greater social efficiency and a more perfect personal freedom. Yet human societies alone keep in full view the needed ends to be obtained.[4]

b) *I possess a mind.* At times man experiences that he lives in a personal body-mind relation. But the question arises: What is the mind?

Man's idea of mind comes from a basic human experience in association with the use of his body and brain. At times one will speak of the *observed mind.* In general, following the possibilities of emphasis, one may really speak of mind in three ways. He may say that the human mind is a material thing. He may say that the mind is a spiritual substance. Or, stressing a duality in unity, he may say that the human individual is one fact, body and mind. The third position suggests that the designations "mental" and "physical" are two aspects of a single organized process.

It is possible to reduce the idea of mind down to a bundle or collection of material particles. Such a theory is associated with a materialistic metaphysics. According to this viewpoint the true nature of each and every entity is but a complex manifestation of its basic element: physical energy. Mind takes place as a function of matter. The subjective experience of mind is said to be an epiphenomenon, a leap in quality, but a totality of material energy. La Mettrie maintained, for example, that animals and men have mental events, but such events are causally dependent on physical activity. Karl Marx maintained that human ideas are the direct emanation of material conduct. Thought, like lightning, would be an electrical discharge. The difficulty in such a reductionist theory is man's living experience of mind. "I experience that I am open to the infinite." As a result, total materialism is as difficult to accept as a total spiritualism.

The second theory is a *brain-mental dualism.* The mind and the brain are two distinct entities but interact causally. Descartes

[4] Ibid., p. 26.

112

formulated his dualistic theory in terms of substances. He was of the opinion that there were two kinds of substances in the universe: mental and corporeal. The essence of a mental substance is that it is a thing that thinks. The essence of a corporeal substance is that it is extended in space. Man is a composite of both substances, so that events in one substance can affect events in the other. Modern dualism, however, tends to say that the mental and the physical are different sorts of events, leaving open the question whether there are real mental substances. One may simply say that the mind changes as mental events occur. An event may be a sort of a thing, a cause, or an effect.

The basic difficulty in any dualistic theory of body and mind comes from the experienced personal unity of man. Mental and physical phenomena appear to be concomitant aspects of a single process of activity. The mind, as in a mind-body dualism, does not appear to be a distinctive entity interacting with matter in the brain.

The third position, at times called a *Metaphysics of Levels*, suggests that the terms "mental" and "physical" are two aspects or levels of a single organized process.

Man is one organic whole with a unified life activity. The unity of man is the fundamental fact. We are able to say, then, that man is embodied mind. At the same time, man experiences himself to be a unified act, with a *transcending* aspect (spirit) and an *embodied* aspect (body or brain). The presence of these diverse levels in the activity of man allows us to attribute two kinds of attributes to a single person: self-consciousness and corporeal interaction.

If one concedes to man a basic unifying activity, then we may say that man acts with his mind and brain. The mind, in this manner of speaking, stresses the subjective level of knowing, while the brain stresses the corporeal activity. Often, from a subjective viewpoint, we speak of mind as man's intuitions, representations, reasoning, and loving. The enlightenment of the subject is a fact. There is an intuition accompanied by evidence associated with the body and brain.

113

When we ask the question, then, what is the mind? the answer appears to be: the mind is the highest *creative activity* in man as embodied. The center of the activity is in the brain. It seems to exercise two basic modes of activity: a causal efficacy over the whole body and a subjective expression power.

In unifying the activity of man, yet preserving the complexity of levels, we are able to avoid that dualism which opposes the interior to the exterior.

c) *I possess a soul*. Man appears to be an essence with a unified total action. At the same time, man experiences himself to be a transcending I, or act. In such a frame of reference, when one says, "I possess a soul," he is referring to a grounding, yet transcending, act. Because of this act he is a subject. "My soul is for me the unique and incomparable reality through which *my* being is rooted in being *itself*."[5]

Such statements do not seem to be metaphysical as such. Rather, they are observations made on the basis of empirical evidence and conscious experience. One is simply saying that man appears to be grounded in an act with transcending aspects. I experience myself as one integrated act with self-conscious awareness. What I perceive in myself, I observe in others. To say that this unifying act is a spiritual substance would be a metaphysical affirmation. An act manifests itself as an act; but to say that this act is a spiritual substance would be pointing to something beyond the act and hidden. As Nietzsche would say, we would be speaking of a world behind the scene.

In living out our human life, we perceive three aspects of the human soul. First, it is the grounding and life giving act of an organic body. Second, its manifestations appear to transcend matter; and it is, as a consequence, a spiritual act. Third, the human act is an act which embodies itself continually.

First. The human soul appears to be a grounding and life giving act. The human person experiences his organic unity and says: "I am"; "I exist." I exist, live and realize myself in and through a

---

[5] Stephan Strasser, *The Soul in Metaphysical and Empirical Psychology*, Pittsburgh Pa.: Duquesne University Press, 1962, p. 106.

114

unifying act or activity. Through man's self-awareness, the act, or process of act, is experienced not as something detached from self or the world but as a presence. The soul, from such a perspective, does not appear to be a thing as such, but an act or presence.

Second. When we interpret the soul as an act through our experience, it discloses itself as a transcending or spiritual presence. As man lives and expresses his continual act of existing, he experiences an inner openness to reality in his self-awareness. He is fully *present* to himself. Through his act of presence he possesses his understanding of reality or truth. In perceiving the intelligibility of reality, he makes value judgments. He makes free choices through personal decisions. In short, not only does the one grounding act unify his organic nature, but it allows him to make constant new transcending acts of knowledge, love, and choice. The grounding act of man, or soul, or spirit, is open to the whole of being and its meaning.

Third. The grounding act or life principle of man embodies itself continually. Though man through his soul seeks to open out beyond himself, at the same time, the soul finds fullness only in embodying itself continually. It informs the body. It gives an organic life to the whole. It is present only in and through the body. It is oriented towards it and towards preserving the unity of man. In this perspective, the soul is a self-embodying act. It makes man to be embodied spirit.

From an empirical mode of knowing, we tend to define man as a living organism. As a living unit he appears to be an energized whole. The basic element seems to be energy, a dynamic act which manifests itself in material quanta or dynamic units. The whole of reality appeals to be a field of inter-related acts.

But what is the basis of all the activity or energy? From an empirical mode of knowing, the temptation is to affirm: matter or material energy.

But when man *experiences* himself through his conscious self-awareness, he confronts a transcending act, or spirit, or soul. From this perspective, though in coherence with his empirical mode of knowing, man confronts himself as possessing a transcending act.

Within himself, he is open to the whole of reality and can intuit its intelligibility. If we now ask the question: What is the basis of all the activity or energy appearing in the universe and in man? the answer appears to be a transcending Act, or Presence, or Power, or Spirit. This Spirit does not seem to be the self-conscious act of man, which idealism suggests as the possible answer. Rather, man seems to be confronting immediately his own act, an embodied act or spirit. The ground of man's spirit does not appear directly. Man always confronts himself and his unified power or energy.

Man's experience of the open transcendence found within himself suggests or points to the possibility that man's act of spirit is grounded in an Act both immanent to him yet transcendent. It is at this juncture of the problem or mystery that man notices a mode of knowing different, yet coherent with his empirical and intuitional experience. This is his *religious* mode of knowing. Man, at times, *experiences* a Holy Presence yet given as a mystery. This mode of knowing—which is a living encounter with the Presence— indicates that a self-conscious Act grounds everything that is. It manifests or discloses itself to the person of man as personal dynamic Power or Spirit.

A Unitary View of Matter and Spirit

Contemporary scientific suppositions, based on some empirical evidence, speak of an evolutionary and unitary view of matter and spirit. According to such a perspective, energy develops and changes into new and higher congealed forms, into living organic units, and, finally, into man as an embodied subject conscious of and to himself. But out of such a general, constructed picture, there rises the question: just what is the difference between living and non-living matter; and, beyond this, between matter and spirit?

An emphasis on the differences appears, as we know, in all dualistic systems of thought. Here one thinks specifically of Plato and Descartes. It is possible, however, while preserving the differences, to emphasize unity. Basically, from this viewpoint, we should emphasize the coherent unity of the whole universe, united together in a shared action and reaction, and evolving organically.

1. Let us analyze any material object in the universe and seek to penetrate into its depths. The object may be a stone, a plant, an animal, a man. If one by visual methods and instruments associated with such a method of knowledge breaks the unity, he perceives, within, a multitude of smaller units that decrease in size and come down to molecules and atoms and then to smaller units which cannot be analyzed. We observe how units of matter are congealed in specific forms and rendered more or less immobile. We are able to observe also the constant dynamic activity. In the process, units appear to break down and disappear, while others seem to act and react; and in doing so, form new units. When we break down a stone, we find congealed energy units. When we break down a plant, an animal, man's body, we find what appears to be live matter in the specific form of cells. We notice some real difference between a stone and the objects with living matter. What is the difference?

The difference between living and non-living matter appears to be one of quality, relation, and event. The difference in quality, as found in living things, refers to the power of unified assimilation, reproduction, heredity, and perception, or some form of consciousness. The difference in relation refers to the law of ever-increasing complexity and inner-concentration found in living things. In such a context, the human brain is the most complicated material thing known and the most concentrated in self-consciousness. The difference of event refers to the uniqueness, the newness, the qualitative leap found in the birth of every living thing out of the potentialities associated with energy.

Empirical evidence combined with human intuitional experience does indicate, then, some real difference between living and non-living things. There appears to be some real difference between living and non-living matter or energy. The statement of difference is not a proven argument as such, but rather, a statement of human awareness. Men are aware of some real difference between living and non-living matter. Arguments can fall to pieces while the awareness remains. Even atoms do not seem to have the same objectivity and concreteness as the living human experience of life as perceived

117

present in plants, animals and man. Yet, though some insight and clarity is achieved through man's conscious perceptions, it is not known how accurately a specific set of concepts describe reality. To what extent is it true to say that the difference between living and non-living matter appears to be one of quality, relation, and event?

We are able to answer this question and difficulty only in terms of a unified act. Matter itself discloses itself in two ways: as a congealed quantity or quantum, and as energy. Living matter discloses itself as any other matter on the level of physics and chemistry; yet, there is disclosed a higher quality, relation, and event, through the presence of a *unifying act*. Nevertheless, the difference between living and non-living matter may seem to be only a question of the complexity of matter in lower plant forms. It is possible to speak of plants as a colony of congealed energy units. This is why, as a way out of the difficulties, one at some point turns to man.

2. Man appears to be a unit of living matter, yet with a transcending *act* or spirit. From the epistemological principle of intuitive self-evidence, or the personal act of understanding found in man, matter does not appear to be spirit or the spirit the matter; rather, there is a living duality in unity. It is in such a context that Thomas Aquinas will say that the soul, "which is the first principle of life, is not a body, but the act of a body,"[6] and then add, "It is clear that man is not only a soul, but something composed of soul and body."[7]

From this viewpoint, man is a unity, an embodied spirit. The emphasis should be placed on the oneness of man. He is one thing: spirit in matter. The spirit is the life principle of the matter, the life giving act of a physical organic body. This spirit or act is experienced to be more than material energy, possessing a transcending intellectual awareness, able to perceive meaning, with an inner self-consciousness.

Man is and remains a mystery. Nevertheless, the answer to the mystery of man does not appear to be in the matter or material

---

[6] *Summa Theologia*, I. q. 75, art. 1.
[7] *Ibid.*, I. q. 75, art. 4.

energy but must be related to the immanent yet transcending act. The empirical and experienced evidence points to a unity of, not opposites, but complementary aspects of reality: body and spirit, body and soul.

According to such an understanding, material energy can and will, under specific circumstances, make a leap into living matter with a unified act, into higher conscious forms, and finally into man. Matter, as one knows it, is energy or power. The life principle in living matter appears to rise out of the creative possibilities inherent in a specific form of matter.

However, when we confront the mystery of man, we state the evidence negatively. The life principle or unifying act is not matter but experienced to be a transcending spirit. The unifying powers in man appear to transcend the properties of matter. The phenomena disclose or manifest the reality. Yet the mystery remains. A materialist may examine the evidence and come to an opposite conclusion: the unifying act in man does not transcend material energy.

3. One added factor should be mentioned. If we interpret the meaning of our world of space and time in terms of our present evidence, though in association with past historical evidence, then the direction of evolving matter and spirit is directed towards the creation of man. Added to this, we perceive that man's deepest self, his personal self consciousness, discloses the meaning and purpose of the whole.

The universe, thus disclosed, is through and through interdependent. The body pollutes the mind, the mind pollutes the body. Physical energy sublimates itself into zeal; conversely, zeal stimulates the body. The biological ends pass into ideals of standards, and the formation of standards affects the biological facts. The individual is formative of the society, the society is formative of the individual. Particular evils infect the whole world, particular goods point the way of escape.[8]

A Christian Understanding of the Unity of Matter and Spirit

The unity of matter and spirit in a human person constitutes a problem which can be answered only by an existential ontology

---

[8] Alfred N. Whitehead, *Religion in the Making*, New York: World Publishing Co., 1971, p. 85.

of self-understanding. The Christian understanding of man is re
lated to such a metaphysics of living awareness; yet, at the same
time, it is related to a *religious experience* accepted as a fact. In a
deep yet true sense, Christianity is a mode of analysis of the actual
world.

1. In the first place, we should notice that the basic Christian
understanding of man is a traditional Jewish viewpoint. Man is
always considered to be a living unity, with a living relationship
to an indwelling yet transcending Spirit (God), the world, and a
co-existence with other men. From such a viewpoint, man is in
no sense a duality; and a given, creative, loving Presence is always
assumed. "When you send forth your Spirit, they are created;
and you renew the face of the ground" (Ps. 104.30). God's creating
Spirit is the foundation of all man is, does, and becomes. Teaching
authorities in the Church have always supported such a conception
of man, adding to the basic Christian experience the affirmation
that the soul is the form of the body (cf., 5th Lateran Council,
1512-1517).

2. The traditional Christian emphasis on the unity of man leads
to the affirmation that God is the immediate Creator of the whole,
saving the lesser creative activity within each and every dynamic
thing. Such a judgment stresses the immanent creating presence of
God in all that pertains to every man. God is the ground of all
man is. His creative Presence is not limited to man's embodied act
or life principle; yet, God creates with the creature. In this perspective, we must not think that God's creative actualization in
man extends only to the soul.

We are then able to understand that man's body is more than a
mere thing yet realize that man becomes human in and through
his body. We are not imprisoned in a body as Platonic thought
supposed; rather, we become man and free human persons in and
through the body. Further, the body mediates to its governing act, or
soul, a knowledge of the outside world and its environment. We need
only think of the mediating function of the eyes and ears. It is the
body which allows us to have real personal relationships with others.

We do not submit to this living relationship of the body with its life principle; rather, man becomes aware of his human condition through his body and learns to accept its burdens and responsibilities. Through our body we become human, exist, and do what must be done in each present moment. As a consequence, *value systems* become directed towards the human. We are able to speak of genuine Christian humanness. We are able to perceive that man is the measure of man and the measure of what he can and should do. We are able to say that man is good to the extent that he acts truly as a human person.

What pertains to the whole body, pertains to our embodied personal consciousness. I possess myself, my body, the world, others, God, through this personal yet embodied consciousness. Here we immediately think of the importance of the brain for the formation of the human person and his ability to know and understand. Yet, at the same moment, we must notice the limitations of the body and the importance of the presence of the power, energy, and act of the spirit. It is the spirit in man that lives, perceives, loves, and hopes.

Further, I am never in complete control of anything, either my embodied self, the world, others, the mystery of God. Rather, man shares his life and creative activity with God and his fellow human beings. We are able to say that we co-exist in a common world. Out of such a mutually shared life or activity man must seek and find his deepest self, be open to reality, be aware of others as unique persons, be compassionate with the mind of Christ, and be free.

3. When we experience the living contrast in man, then, out of self-transcending awareness, we affirm that the life principle in man, soul, act, or spirit, makes a man to be person. I am a man because of my spirit. I am more than material energy. I experience myself to be spirit through a self-awareness and understanding. I represent this experience through my ideas or concepts. I objectify my experience of spirit through my life with my body, by what I do in the world, and in constructing community. Yet such a Christian

understanding of the human soul, as informing life giving personal subjectivity, must not imply that the soul is pure spirit. The human soul, as we experience and know man, designates at some point embodied existence.

4. Such a strange unity of matter and spirit constitutes the problem of man. We experience ourself to be one unified act of existing, not two. Yet, we perceive the living duality. Man is embodied spirit. Every act or activity in man is embodied. Such an embodied existence pertains to the total actuality of man and his presence to himself and others. It is our unified awareness, that tells us that matter and spirit in man are not two things but, rather, two complementary aspects of man. The body is not a part of man; neither is the spirit. Rather, man is an embodied act.

Such an understanding of man, as embodied act, extends to all the aspects and horizons of human existence. This means that the human body is a living expression of the soul, its sign and manifestation. We disclose who and what we are through our body in speaking, knowing, loving, at work or play, co-existing with others. The soul, or the unifying act in man, can express the mystery of what it is as spirit only through the body. This explains why people need to live with others and talk to them, why people in love tend to embrace each other, why religious manifestations in man need to be objectified in prayers with sound, through signs, and community liturgy.

5. To perceive that man is embodied spirit or act, allows us to understand what is meant by the Christian affirmation that Jesus is, truly and uniquely, God-man. If man is embodied spirit, grounded in Spirit, or God, then Jesus is the perfection of the possibilities found in man.

For one thing, this doctrine of the Hypostatic Union, understood in its truly Catholic sense (i.e., according to the teaching of Chalcedon), has nothing mythical about it. It is clearly not mythology to say that God's infinity is given to me in the absolute transcendence of the spirit, and that—since something is real according to the measure of its being by itself and by the absolute infinity of being—this presence of God is more actual and real than the reality of any finite thing. No more is it mythology to say that self-transcendence (which in us consists in principle always merely in becoming and beginning), has reached an absolute and insurpassable climax in a determinate man, who is an absolutely real man in every way—a man with a human consciousness, with free will and historicity, who worships and obeys and experiences the torments of death; in whom God's communication of himself to the spiritual nature of the creature took place in a unique and unsurpassable manner. It is not mythology to say—there is a man by reason of whose existence I may dare to believe that God has promised to give himself irrevocably and finally to me; there is a man in whom God's absolute promise to give himself to every spiritual creature, and the acceptance of this promise by the creature, are both proved and rendered credible to me without ambiguity, irreparably and in a manner I can understand.[9]

If man is embodied spirit, then Jesus is the perfection of this and its ultimate possibility. If man is grounded in Spirit, or God, then Jesus is the perfection of this and its ultimate possibility. To this we are able to add that God became man uniquely and perfectly in one man to give us a new life beyond death in and through a salvation that embraces our body.

---

[9] Karl Rahner, *Theological Investigations*, vol. 5, p. 11-12.

Chapter 7

Nature and Grace

General Observations

The expression 'nature and grace' is a traditional representation, or formula, pointing to the mystery of man as he confronts in his person or in community with others the creating Presence of God. In such a basic framework, the term 'nature' designates man and the term 'grace' designates God as a loving and life-giving Act. From a traditional Christian perspective the formula sums up the experienced belief that God creates man for a shared personal life in and with himself; and this sharing—or living personal relationship—is made effectual or real in each man's existence by God's creative Presence rather than from anything found in man himself. Man, however, as a free subject, may respond in many diverse ways, according to his sensed awareness and engaged responsibility. Further, he may express his experience from many viewpoints but always in an historical context.

The question or problem is: How does man come to perceive such a gracious Presence out of his self-understanding or self-awareness?

Man's Self-Awareness and his Experience of God

What are we directly aware of with our self-consciousness? The answer, based on our self-understanding, appears to be: we confront directly our act of being. We are conscious of ourself as embodied act. Through added attention, reflecting on the transcending tendencies of this act, we speak of ourself as embodied spirit. These tendencies are experienced to be open to the infinite. At the same time we are aware that we do not confront an infinite Spirit directly or, as it is said, face to face. It is because of this limitation of man's direct self-awareness that any living confrontation with a grounding personal Presence within ourself must come to us as a gift or grace. God must disclose himself to us through the mediation of our experience, though we must be attentive. He calls to us and we respond.

From a natural viewpoint, it is always possible for us to think and say that we are grounded in material energy or in Spirit; that we are grounded either in a Nothingness, an Emptiness, or infinite Fullness. We experience ourself as a mystery; and out of this situation come our conflicting opinions, doubts, and temptations.

Again, once we perceive that our knowledge of God is mediated through experience, then we notice two added factors pertaining to our awareness. First, from a subjective aspect, or our human manner of knowing, our knowledge of God can be mediated through our empirical knowledge, through our intellectual insights, and from our religious experience. Second, from an objective aspect, our knowledge of God is mediated through our living relations to the world in which we live, through our life with our fellow men, and through our constant living relationship to the grounding Presence within. As Buber would say, this relationship is clouded, yet it discloses itself as a Thou. Further, every disclosure of a person comes to us as a grace.

The awakening of our person in our self-awareness, or knowledge, in relationship to the world, others, and the mysterious Other, discloses our finiteness, the meaninglessness of human life, and our dissatisfactions. There arises a longing for a perfected relationship between our self and the world, others, and the Mystery. We are never content with the measure or degree of the developed relations which allow us to survive and master the needs of our daily life. A higher longing or love always appears. In it the genuineness of the person becomes manifest. Human love is not the mere performance of duty but the earnest affirmation of the person which must be offered in our living relations.

Man's experience of himself and of the grounding Mystery within himself is reflected upon and interpreted within the meaningful context of his world and his relationships with other persons. Often, then, when we speak of man's experience of God, we are referring to his extended relationships with the world, others, and the Mystery within, ranging over a lifetime. The basic human experience appears to be a common shared awareness, yet unique for each person because qualified by specific things, events, and particular persons. We speak of the particular history of a particular person (the God of Abraham, Isaac and Jacob) or of a particular group of people (Hinduism, Buddhism, Judaism, Christianity, Catholicism).

Since we encounter the Mystery God through the mediation of our human experience, we are able to say that the foundation of our religious awareness is associated with our transcendental tendencies and acts of knowing and loving, in freedom. God on his part confronts our spirit through his creating Act or Spirit. Basically we confront this grounding Spirit in an unthematic manner. We say that we confront a Mystery who calls to us through the medium of a Word and as a loving Power or Thou. Through our life experiences and personal reflections we thematize, represent, and objectify the deeper intelligibility in human acts of knowing, loving, with a given personal freedom.

The Biblical Understanding of Grace

Since our living experience of the mystery of Spirit who grounds and approaches us as a creating Act is related to our knowledge of the world and others, our religious experience always falls within an historical horizon. We live, in some real way, out of the traditions that come to us from the past.

In general, from a Biblical viewpoint, God must always disclose his Presence. God goes out to meet man. Yet the disclosure takes place in a divine and human confrontation. In such a context, the expression 'nature and grace' refers to living personal relationships. The gift of God's gracious Presence is one of liberation. He gives to man a constant, yet ever new, free life. Man's experience of the need of wholeness seems to demand this gift for his peace.

1. The Old Testament writings, which are the objectification of the spiritual experience of the Jewish community, have no particular word to designate what the New Testament calls *charis*, or grace. Yet its whole message is that genuine human life depends on personal faith and that the blessings of life are gift given.

In this general context, the Septuagint translates the Hebrew term *chen*, which means the good will, the affection, the kindness or active favor of one in a higher position (cf., Ps. 45.2), with the Greek term *charis*. From the point of view of the Mystery, God, as he discloses himself in his personal relationships with Israel, is a loving Presence. He regards men with kindness and bestows on them his free favors. In this relationship, God always takes the initiative. He acts the way he does because of what he is, a loving Presence, rather than what man is. The special election of Israel rests on such a kindness and favor. The historical event and symbol of God's graciousness is the Exodus.

It was not because you were more in number than any other people that the Lord set his love upon you and chose you, for you were the fewest of all peoples; but it was because the Lord loves you, and is keeping the oath which he swore to your fathers, that the Lord has brought you out with a mighty hand, and redeemed you from the house of bondage, from the hand of the Pharaoh king of Egypt.[1]

God is experienced to be rich in *chesed*, a union of faithfulness, loving kindness, or steadfast love. Often the terms *chesed* and *emeth* are joined together to form the idea of a faithful union that is indissoluble. God's *chesed* is both habitual and active, looking towards the overcoming of human sins through a forgiveness which has an effect on a person's life. "A new heart I will give you, and a new spirit I will put within you" (Ezek. 36.26). God's *chesed* gives man a new life in freedom, justice, and peace. At the same time, the perfection of God's loving Presence is to be found in the life of a man's spirit. God's Spirit bears witness to our spirit.

The succinct statement 'for thy steadfast love is better than life' (Ps. lxiii.4 (3)) gives a glimpse of how fundamentally the relative importance of all values had changed, for normally life and its enhancement through Jahweh's

---

[1] Deut. 7.7-8. Cf., also: C. Ryder Smith, *The Bible Doctrine of Grace*, London, 1956, p. 8ff.

blessing was at all times the highest of good things for Israel. This discrimination between loving kindness and life was something wholly new: it signified the discovery of the spiritual as a reality beyond the frailty of the corporeal. This faith no longer had need of anything external, neither the saving history nor objective rites, for Jahweh's salvation appertained to it from within itself.[2]

From the expressed religious experience and understanding of ancient Israel, God himself is grace. He is experienced to be a loving Presence both in himself and in his acts. At the same time, God's favors or blessings, always associated in some context with man's life, may be said to be graces, though in a secondary sense. They come to man out of God's loving fidelity. In some real way, the whole of creation may be said to be graced. The perfection of such grace or favor is to be found in a man's living relationship with Yahweh. "For with thee is the fountain of life; and in thy light do we see light." (Ps. 36.10). In his loving Presence, Yahweh breaks in on a man's life, calls to him, questions him in such a manner that he questions himself, rules over him, promises new blessings in the future, and gives him peace. In this graciousness, Yahweh makes man come into himself and live through his earthly existence, for He calls to him in relationship with everything.

When one reads the Old Testament, one reservation should be noted. The Hebrew mentality never seeks to explain the mystery of God's graciousness through set words and thoughts. Rather, at his best, a person sought to confront the living God in his own existence, in the context of history, and in reference to the future. Such an understanding, as one can perceive, stresses subjective experience. On the objective side, one confronts a creating Presence. God is experienced to be the creating Ground and Lord of all things.

2. When one turns to the New Testament writings, we notice that these are an objectification, in a general manner, of the same Jewish experience. One still confronts the gracious God in his own personal existence, through a new mediating Presence: Jesus Christ. The confrontation takes place in the context of history as there is good news about God's present activity. Again, one expects and

---

[2] Gerhard von Rad, *Old Testament Theology*, New York: 1962, vol. 1, p. 403.

awaits for the fulfillment of the new life, or way, in the future. From the objective side, there is a new creation. But here one is moving into the ancient Greek and Roman worlds. When one speaks of grace, one speaks of *charis,* a Greek word designating loveliness, charm, graciousness. In the context of personal relationships, *charis* indicates a giving of one's self, a kindness, good will, or a thankfulness and gratitude. In the New Testament writings, then, *charis,* or grace, carries with its use all the tones of meaning associated with a Greek understanding, yet representing the religious experience of New Israel. *Charis* as used in the New Testament refers to a life of salvation in and with God but experienced through the loving and serving Presence of Jesus Christ. Matthew's gospel in its final affirmation has Jesus say: "I am with you always, to the close of the age" (Matt. 28.20).

Basically, the New Testament writings are a description of man's experience of God in and through the mediating person and power (Spirit) of Jesus. One comes to an awareness of God's creating and loving Presence and the interior gifts associated with this Presence. In such a context, Paul the Apostle writes to the Romans: "Grace to you and peace from God the Father and our Lord Jesus Christ" (Rom. 1.3). Grace, fundamentally, is God's creating and loving Act or Presence, but with diverse aspects as it touches one's personal relationships with men. It can manifest itself as Word or Spirit. As it affects man, it may have great existential and social variability. It may be refused and called rejected grace.

In so far as the New Testament writings express a theology of *creation,* with God considered a *creating* Presence, every statement about God speaks of his grace extended towards man; and, in turn, every statement about man is also a statement about God's creating and gracious Presence. But, more specifically, the New Testament speaks about a new creating and gracious Presence that takes place in and through the Person and Spirit of Jesus Christ. Paul the Apostle will say that he is speaking about the good news that comes through a revelation of Jesus Christ (Gal. 1.12). God is experienced as addressing man through a new mediating Presence. The Apostle declares, speaking about an event or events pertaining to his own life, that God has called to him through his grace and revealed his Son to him (Gal. 1.15-16). Traditionally, theology speaks of a new and final reign of God through Christ, the *regnum Christi*. Paul will say in his own way that Christ is the power of God and the wisdom of God (1 Cor. 1.24). John will say that this creating and addressing incarnate Word is full of grace and truth (Jn. 1.14). Luke will say, speaking of the primitive Christian community, that we are saved through the grace of the Lord Jesus (Acts 15.11).

In the context of a creation theology, the New Testament declares that a new work of God's grace is taking place in history and men's lives through the mediating Presence of the dead and risen Jesus. "For in him all the fullness of God was pleased to dwell and through him to reconcile to himself all things, whether on earth or in heaven, making peace by the blood of the cross" (Col. 1.19-20).

The theme of God's creating and gracious Presence can be experienced and explained in many different ways. The Old and New Testament writings explain it existentially and within an historical context. It can also be explained in terms of being, or reality, in an ontological theology. One can also explain it in terms of immanence and transcendence. It can also be considered and explained in relation to Nothingness. Here one thinks almost immediately of the philosophy of Jean-Paul Sartre and his work, *Being and Nothingness*. God is No-Thing.

Justification

God as a creating Presence in ancient Israel was experienced to be *holy* and *just*. He is the All Holy, the Holy One of Israel. He does not create in chaos (cf., Is. 45.18). He does not say to his people, "Seek me in chaos" (cf., Is. 45.19). Rather, he demands: "You shall be to me a kingdom of priests and a holy nation" (Ex. 19. 6). The people must be holy before the Lord and just among themselves. As the creating Presence, God is the norm. He declares what is just (cf., Is. 45.19). In such a perspective, a man may be said to be good and just, not strictly for what he is in himself, but because he is grounded in the creating power of God and subject to his judgment and approval (cf., Is. 45.24).

Such a point of view, as one can observe, is related to God's creative Presence in the world. God is experienced to be holy and the norm for man's activity. God creates in an orderly manner. This suggests that man should act in the same way, which in the framework of society and political life indicates the pressing demands of love and justice. God's judgment and approval become manifest in the events of history.

Love, however, is deeply personal and knows no set laws. It can only be manifested in new ways. Justice, however, since it regulates proper order in society and among people, takes specific forms in law norms. Justice, furthermore, can be manifested in one person: the just judge. From this viewpoint, just laws are a manifestation of God's immanent Presence in the world. They specify in a particular way the demands of God's love and justice.

In the Old Testament, as a consequence, God is imaged out as a judge, a king-judge of antiquity who commands a control over human life. "Righteous are you, O Lord, when I complain to you; yet I would plead my case before you" (Jer. 12.1). Man, as he has been created by God is good but human. He fails constantly, day by day, in the proper relationships or order that should exist between himself and his world, others, and his sovereign Lord. Yet he must receive God's approval or acceptance. "Hear my prayer, O Lord; give ear to my supplications. In your faithfulness answer me, in your righteousness. Enter not into judgment with your servant; for no man living is righteous before you" (Ps. 143. 1-2). God's judgment of approval in the context of a man's human life is one of freeing action. God gives man an experience of the divine steadfast love but in the form of mercy and forgiveness. "In your righteousness bring me out of trouble. And in your steadfast love cut off my enemies" (Ps. 143. 11-12).

In the New Testament God's justice is the same as it is in the Old Testament. It is God's creative and loving Presence ruling in the work of creation, in men, and in the shared lives of men. Yet, God can and does manifest his righteousness in specific forms. One

131

can still perceive the basic nature of God's action when he looks at a king-judge. God's judgment is a freeing action, an act of liberation, disclosed to man in the midst of his sins, weaknesses, and failings. The new manifestation is the incarnation of God's Son, or Word, his life, death, and resurrection. Man on his part has a living experience of God's steadfast love and justice which, again, is one of mercy and forgiveness. This general picture shines through the words of Paul the Apostle:

The love of Christ controls us, because we are convinced that one has died for all; therefore all have died. And he died for all that those who live might live no longer for themselves but for him who for their sake died and was raised.
From now on, therefore, we regard no one from a human point of view; even though we once regarded Christ from a human point of view, we regard him thus no longer. Therefore, if any one is in Christ, he is a new creation; the old has passed away, behold, the new has come. All this is from God, who through Christ reconciled us to himself and gave us the ministry of reconciliation; that is, God was in Christ reconciling the world to himself, not counting their trespasses against them, and entrusting to us the message of reconciliation.[3]

From the general perspective of a creation theology, we may simply say that God is manifesting his creating and loving Presence in the universe in a new manner and through the mediating, yet creating, Presence of the dead and risen Jesus. He is experienced to be a mediating Presence in and with God.

Yet, obviously, one may look at this experienced good news in a specific form. One can look at God as a king-judge who has pronounced a verdict of justice, mercy, reconciliation, for all men through the death and resurrection of Jesus. Man may leave court rather than go to prison or die. He has the right, with the needed possibilities, to a full human life in freedom. However, he must respond by faith. Paul, the apostle, speaks within this framework of understanding when he writes:

There is no distinction, since all have sinned and fall short of the glory of God, they are justified by his grace as a gift, through the redemption which is in Christ Jesus, whom God put forward as an expiation by his blood, to be received by faith. . . . This was to show God's righteousness

---

[3] 2 Cor. 5.14-19.

132

because in his divine forbearance he had passed over former sins; it was to prove at the present time that he himself is righteous and that he justifies him who has faith in Jesus.[4]

Obviously, then, one can and may speak of God's gracious and justifying Presence among men in legal and forensic terms. Further, particular difficulties with such an explanation can be resolved within the framework of a broader *creation theology*. We perceive the resolution of particular difficulties taking place in the theological explanations given by Paul, the apostle.

The religious experience of ancient Israel immediately associated with historical events, allowed them to affirm that God is a creating and loving Presence who had entered into a unique I-Thou relationship with the community. In this relationship Israel was a new creation, God's special people. Israel's moral experience was of a Presence who was holy, loving, just. Man in responding to God must also be holy, loving and just. But a difficulty was to be found in specific moral and legal laws or commands. Where did they come from? Often the assumption was that they came directly from God since he is the Lord and king of his people. God creates and rules over all things, not through chaos, but through order. This genuine human situation with its problems appeared in Israel at least from 1000 B.C. onward. One was caught in a web of laws. The man who fulfills the Mosaic Law is just. One justifies and sanctifies himself by the exact fulfillment of divine legislation.

Paul as a pharisee had accepted the commonly shared opinion that a man's justification before God comes from a personal observance of law. God gives the legal precepts. A man must accomplish his own justification. The apostle spoke of this understanding as a justification through the law (Gal. 2.21).

Paul understood this theological tradition within his personal historical situation. He had been educated as a pharisee and served God according to a fixed pattern. One becomes good, holy, just, in fulfilling the demands of the *Torah*. In becoming a Christian he realizes that man as a creature is subject to God's personal call rather than to fixed laws or structures. God called to him through his

---

[4] Rom. 3:22-26.

grace and revealed his Son to him (Gal. 1.15-16). He experiences in his own person and life the love of Christ. He has become a new creation, a new man. He realizes now that a man is justified before God not through the observance of particular laws as such, though he understands the value of such norms, but by a total living response to God. "A man is not justified by works of the law but through faith in Jesus Christ" (Gal. 2.16). "It is no longer I who live, but Christ who lives in me; and the life I now live in the flesh I live by faith in the Son of God, who loved me and gave himself for me" (Gal. 2.20). The death and resurrection of Jesus are signs of God's new creative Presence. These are living signs, because Jesus remains in a condition of death yet alive as the risen Lord. Besides his ruling influence over a man's human existence and religious experience, Jesus also is present in the Christian community through the principal signs of Baptism and the Eucharist.

Within this framework we are able to say that Christianity gives an existential, mystical, and sacramental explanation of man's encounter with God. Such an explanation is opposed to any simple juridical and ethical understanding. The world of man is good in itself yet a tension of conflicting powers. Creation, order, continuity, love, justice, and peace come into the whole of history through God's grace.

The Understanding of God's Grace in Christian Antiquity

Christianity as a shared human experience is a life with God in and through the mediating Presence of Jesus. Such an awareness can be called, as Nietzsche suggested, an illusion of a world behind the scene. To this a Christian can only reply that he experiences a personal Mystery who calls to him with a loving power. The Mystery addresses him through the medium of a Word and in Spirit. The addressing Word is experienced to be the living Jesus. The Spirit appears to be the Spirit of Jesus or his loving Presence.

In some real way, a person's religious experience is problematic. One confronts a Mystery, and the awareness is of a light shining in darkness. At some point one declares, "I live by faith." But the awareness is a shared experience and the light is represented in diverse manners of speaking, from many viewpoints, and in an historical context. In such a frame of reference, a Christian recognizes and declares that his knowledge of God is in some real manner mediated through the community. The community as such not only has a present but also a past. We live out of the traditions that come to us.

We should observe, however, that the answer of faith is always given in the context of problems that arise in a particular world. Again, man faces his problems of understanding in the context of the development of the human mind and answers to a large extent within the framework of ruling philosophical systems of thought. At the same time, God's freedom calls to each human person, demanding his responsible answer. One is free to answer with a "Yes" or "No," with faith or unbelief, with the church or in opposition to it.

1. *Stoic and Platonic Influence.* As the Christian community developed and took its place in a Greek and Roman world, its basic Judaic and Christian ideas became associated with Stoic and Platonic horizons of thought.

Clement of Rome (c. 96 A.D.) proclaims that we have "one God and one Christ and one Spirit of grace shed upon us" (Ep. to the Cor. 46.6). We "are not justified through ourselves or through our own wisdom or understanding or piety, or our actions done in holiness of heart, but through faith; for it is through faith that Almighty God has justified all" (*Ibid.*, 32). Yet he speaks like a Stoic, saying: "Let us put on concord, being humble in mind, disciplined, keeping ourselves from gossip and slander, being justified by works, not words" (*Ibid.*, 30). Holiness is associated with the quality of human life rather than with personal relationships. At the same time, the Christian is to be attentive to an ideal Platonic world: "Through him (Christ) let us gaze fixedly into the heights of heaven" (*Ibid.*, 36).

Ignatius of Antioch (c. 118) speaks of Jesus as being the life of the Christian. He dwells within each of us and is the source of our immortality. We are God-bearers and Christ-bearers. We live and act with Christ. Without him we cannot have a genuine human life. "There is only one physician, a physician who is at once flesh and spirit, generate and ingenerate, God in man, true life in death, born of Mary and of God, first passible then impassible, Jesus Christ our Lord" (Ep. to the Ephesians, 7).

In the 2nd and 3rd centuries, the Apologists gave their immediate attention to the defense of Christianity. The emphasis is Platonic. Christianity is true and good. Justin Martyr will say: "I found only this philosophy is safe and useful" (Dial. 8). What Plato and the Stoics say coheres with the teachings of the Christians. "Each, through his share in the divine generating Logos, speaks well, perceiving what was suited to his capacity" (Apologia II. 13). Christ is the intelligible principle or Logos, immanent in God, who took upon himself an incarnate existence. He is the living teacher of the human race giving to the Christians a deeper knowledge (*gnosis*) and wisdom. Irenaeus teaches that in Jesus the divine Logos entered uniquely into human nature by becoming incarnate. He is the new Adam who begins a new life or mankind. He offers us the Spirit of God that we may live a holy life in good works and obtain immortality.

In general, we may say, early Christianity attempted to harmonize what it believed with Stoic and Platonic insight. In agreement with Stoic thought, Jesus is the intelligible Principle, or Logos, grounding all things. This Logos became incarnate in Jesus. In agreement with Platonic insight, Christianity seeks after the perfection of the true and good. This is accomplished in a person's life with the Logos and Spirit of God dwelling within. As Irenaeus affirms (Adv. Haer. 5, 27, 2): "Fellowship with God is light and life. Separation from God is death."

2. *The Theology of Alexandria and the East.* In the 3rd century, the catechetical school of Alexandria, in Egypt, sought to create a living synthesis between Jewish and Greek thought. Men were invited to seek after a higher knowledge (*gnosis*) which was at the same time a knowledge shared with the Logos (Word of God)

and in community with others, a Christian gnosis. The first proponents of this way of thinking and living were Clement of Alexandria (c. 150-c. 215) and Origen (c. 185-c. 254). In general, Eastern Christian theology developed out of the possibilities inherent in the thought of Origen. The dynamic Presence of the Logos in all things is the central idea.

Clement of Alexandria maintains that all things are grounded in an Almighty Power or Presence, the *Pantokrator*. From man's experience of life and reality, it is exceedingly difficult for him to discover the First Cause of anything and to describe the Supreme Cause. God is not a thing and exists without form. We call him One, Good, Mind, Existence, Father, God, Creator, Lord, in order that our thought may have a specific idea to rest upon. Taken singly, however, such terms do not express the being of God, though collectively, they point to the Grounding Presence, the Pantokrator.

This Unknown, whom we address as Thou, is really known by divine grace and the Word, or Logos, proceeding from God (Cf., *Stromateis*, Bk. 5). We cannot believe in the Son, or Logos, without truly knowing who and what he is. "Faith is not without knowledge as the Father is not without the Son." Faith comes in through the ears of the soul. There is a common faith which all believers possess and this proceeds from faith to faith. Such a faith is like a grain of mustard seed which stings the soul into life and then develops according to God's grace. The Spirit of the incarnate Logos is a light or lamp which searches out the depths of what each man is.

Origen, much like Clement of Alexandria, is a biblical theologian. At the same time, somewhat like Plotinus, he represents and expresses his ideas with the framework of Platonic philosophy. Origen constructed a unified theology of the Logos.

The four gospels express, in the opinion of Origen, the shared religious experience, or *gnosis*, of the Christian community. Again, what the church experiences was stated by the affirmation of Paul the Apostle (2 Cor. 5. 19): "God was in Christ reconciling the whole world to himself" (Com. on John, Bk. 1, 6). Jesus is the incarnate Logos or the expressed Word of God. As such, he is the mediating Presence in all things. He is the way, the truth, and life. He is the light of the world, the door, the good shepherd of all things, the source of man's resurrection, the alpha and omega. When the intelligibility of this is expressed in one's words, we find external Christianity. When its meaning is disclosed in man's action, we find spiritual Christianity (*Ibid.*, Bk. 1). Jesus, then, as the incarnate Logos, is the creating Ground of everything. He is the source of all life. He is the expressed light of God; and as such, he is the Principle of man's knowledge and love. In him, each man receives and finds sanctification and redemption. The end purpose of the creating power of the Logos in each man is to establish a living communion between the person and God, so that man might become in some real manner divine (cf., Contra. Celsus, 3. 28). The Platonic idea of the divinization of man has been given a Christian interpretation.

From the viewpoint of Origen, Jesus is the incarnate Logos; and, in dying and rising again, passed into a higher and new life in God. Jesus, as the incarnate Logos or Word is present in all things. He is present in each man as a mediating Presence. He mediates man's living communion with God. The divinization process is one of shared life. We have, as a result, a theology of the incarnate Word rather than one of the Cross.

Origen, as the theologian of the incarnate Word, is the Father of Eastern Christian thought, though one could follow him in a form of biblicism, cosmic ontology, or idealism. The East has for the most part accepted the incarnation theology of Origen, while questioning his ontology and idealism.

3. *The Theology of the West.* Pelagianism in the 5th century reduced the meaning of the term grace (*gratia*) to the natural perfections found in man's nature. Grace was the good in man's nature as a whole; or, if one considered the specific perfections found in man's nature, it is his endowment with reason and free will. The perfection of man's nature with its abilities (the *posse*) comes from God. The will to use such perfections (the *velle*) and the acts (the

esse) come from man. Said another way, grace according to Pelagius is the "gift of possibility" that man has received.[5]

St. Augustine (354-430) reacted to the position of Pelagius. In his mind, Pelagius had reduced a much wider whole down to a part and confused man's nature with grace. Pelagius had given a natural interpretation of man's life. If one maintains that appearances manifest the whole of reality, then it seems true to say that we have been thrown into existence and into a specific world. It is for each man to will and act. But this is an answer from first appearances. Augustine looked deeper into man through his intellectual insights and religious experience. He perceived in man a union of the finite and infinite. God grounded man in all he was and did. God acts and man cooperates (*illo operante cooperamur*).

From the viewpoint of Augustine, God most uniquely is grace. In his sense, it is God's creating power in man, or God's Spirit.[6] God himself is uncreated grace. He is the transcendent source of all being, truth, and goodness. Augustine, however, thinks within a Neo-Platonic perspective. He is not thinking in terms of personal communion but from the view of *creative act*. God acts in man in all he is and does that man may cooperate. God's creative act illumines man's intellect from within. God's creative act makes man's will good and gives the will the power or potential to do good. Human ignorance is overcome by God's light. The love of self and human lust are overcome by God's infused love. God's creative act, in so far as it achieves its proper effect, may be called *predestinating* grace. We find the general position of Augustine stated in his *City of God:*

The spirit of life, therefore, which quickens all things, and is the creator of every body, and of every created spirit, is God himself, the uncreated spirit. In His supreme will resides the power which acts on the wills of all created spirits, helping the good, judging the evil, controlling all, granting power to some, not granting it to others. For, as He is the creator of all natures, so also is He the bestower of all powers, not of all

---

[5] Cf., *Documents of the Christian Church*, ed. by Henry Bettenson, New York: Oxford Press, 1947, p. 75. Cf., also Reihold Seeberg, *The History of Doctrines*, Baker, Michigan, 1966, p. 336ff.

[6] Cf., R. Seeberg, op. cit., p. 341ff.

wills; for wicked wills are not from Him, being contrary to nature, which is from Him.[7]

Augustine maintained, as one may observe from his statement, that there could be opposition between God's creative act (grace) and man's nature. God is the source of being, truth, and goodness; but not of evil. An evil does not come from God. Hence, in speaking about the gift of perseverance, he will write, "He who falls, falls by his own will; he who stands, stands by the will of God" (*Gift of Perseverance*, 8.19). Such an implied opposition between God's creating act (grace) and man's existing nature will create many theological problems in the future.

Thomas Aquinas (1225-1274) followed, in general, the opinions of St. Augustine in his theology of grace but mediated such insights through reality, or being, using the system of Aristotle. In such a framework, reality or being, is always good. Anything is good to the extent that it is. As a consequence, man in his nature is good. Evil, to the contrary, is not being or reality as such; rather, evil is a deprivation of some particular good that should be present in a particular thing. It can only be defined in reference to reality or the good; yet it is always a lack of the good. Physical evil is the lack of the good order proper to a particular thing. Moral evil is the lack of due order which is proper to a human act: a defect in knowledge, in love, in the act itself, or in the purpose. Realism seeks after human understanding (*intetellectus*) as the intellect pierces into the depths of reality. Since its insights are mediated through set terms associated with a system of reality, *Nominalism* will protest at some point that such terms are the creation of the human spirit and one is caught up in no more than a language game. To this objection Thomas Aquinas replies that objective ideas are, most certainly, created representations of the human mind, yet possess a foundation in reality, and so point to reality. At the same time, Thomas Aquinas, like Paul the apostle and St. Augustine, is living and thinking out of his religious experience. Nevertheless, since man does not know God as he is in himself, God's Presence is mediated through being.

---

[7] Augustine, *City of God*, Bk. 5, ch. 9.

In such a general framework of thinking, Thomas speaks of grace in terms of being. The term Grace, he says, refers to something supernatural in man coming to him from God.[8] Grace may be God himself, the life of the soul; or it may be an effect in the soul: either a gift or favor freely given, or the reception and acceptance of the gift.[9]

In so far as a man is moved by God either to know or will, this gratuitous effect is a movement of the soul, *motus quidam animae*. Augustine had said the same while using different terms. He had said that God acts in the soul and man cooperates. Thomas speaks in the terms of Aristotle. The effect, or the grace, in the soul is said to be a motion of the soul. The soul is moved, yet reacts as a free agent. Such a motion may be said to be actual grace.

From the perspective of man's reconciliation with God, Thomas maintains that a man's life with God comes to him from grace. Grace is never a matter of right. This is looking at man from the point of view of what he is. But to the extent that a man cooperates, or lives in union with God (habitual grace), he may be said to merit eternal life condignly or out of a fitting worthiness (*meritum de condigno*).[10]

From the viewpoint of Thomist theology, as one can observe, the term *nature*, refers to human nature as such, or what it means to be a man; the term *grace* refers to a reality that comes to man because of God's favor or gift. The intelligibility of such terms may, and can be, represented within the framework of ontology. Yet grace always remains grace. We may look on it as the traditional Catholic viewpoint supported by authority. It may be questioned from the standpoint of Nominalism as a system of subjective rationalism. One has done no more than project his own thoughts. It may be questioned from the standpoint of faith as an illusionary ontology based on the analogy of being. It may also be questioned by any Christian when it appears as a *power-system* requiring sub-

---

[8] Thomas Aquinas, *Summa Theologiae*, I, II, q. 110, art. 1: "Sic igitur per hoc quod dicitur homo gratiam Dei habere, significatur quidem supernaturale in homine a Deo proveniens.

[9] Cf., *Summa*, I, II, q. 109-113.

[10] Ibid., I, II, q. 114, art. 3.

mission to authority rather than to the living God. The questioning begins with the Protestant reformation.

The Understanding of God's Grace
at the Time of the Reformation

The reformation movement of the 16th century may be considered generally as a reaction against an ontological theology and a dogmatic theology resting on teaching authority. Christians protested in the name of faith and God's Word. The cry became: "Faith alone!" "God's Word!" "Scripture alone!" The counter cry was: "Faith and reason!" "Faith and works!" "Scripture and tradition!"

The problem is one of coherence and wholeness, which in human life is sought for and found in a tension of contraries. At times, the conflict is called the struggle between institutional and free Christianity. The local church of Rome, it would appear, had a double foundation due to the Petrine and Pauline missions. Peter was the Apostle to Israel, while Paul was the Apostle to the Gentiles, proclaiming a free gospel apart from the Law. These two apostles represent two basic streams in Christianity which are at times antithetical. The problem is to live with Peter *and* Paul.

1. *The Theology of Martin Luther (1483-1546).* Luther was a biblical theologian and his basic Christian understanding is set forth in his *Lectures on Paul's Epistle to the Romans* and his commentary on the *Epistle to the Galatians* (1535). He explained his viewpoint more specifically in his preaching and disputations. He had an open bias against Aristotle and the power of human reason, a bias which can be understood in the light of his personal background. At times he thought by way of antithesis of confronting Law with the Gospel. Specifically, the theology of Luther may be summed up in two affirmations: first, "Christ reigns through grace"; second, "Spiritual birth is nothing other than faith."[11]

How does Christ reign over us? The dead and risen Christ mediates God's saving Presence. "Christ gives grace and peace not

---

[11] Cf., *Lectures on Galations* (1535), found in *Luther's Works* St. Louis: Concordia Publishing House, 1963, vol. 26, p. 445-6.

as the apostles did, by preaching the gospel, but as its author and Creator. The Father creates and gives life, grace, peace, etc.; the Son creates and gives the very same things. To give grace, peace, eternal life, the forgiveness of sins, justification, life, and deliverance from death and the devil—these are the works, not of any creature but only of the Divine Majesty."[12] Christ as a mediating Presence lives, acts, and speaks in each man. The Christian experiences Christ as present and active in his life.

How does a man live by faith? He experiences within himself the mediating Presence of Christ. In this context, Christ is said to be the form (*forma*) of faith. "The true Gospel is this: Works or love are not the ornament of perfection of faith; but faith itself is a gift of God, a work of God in our hearts, which justifies us because it takes hold of Christ as the Savior."[13]

Such a living experience of Christ through God's Spirit awakens in man a real inner justice or righteousness, a *justitia interior*. In our life, however, this inner justice is never perfect or complete. It is always subject to change and development. As a result, man is always a sinner yet justified—*justus et peccator*—possessing contrary orientations. He is both spiritual and carnal, just and sinner, good and evil. "Thus a Christian man is righteous and a sinner at the same time, holy and profane, an enemy of God and a child of God. None of the sophists will admit this paradox, because they do not understand the true meaning of justification."[14]

Luther's statements on grace and man's justification are, basically, experiential affirmations. Guided by the New Testament writings, he spoke as he experienced human life with God in and through the risen Jesus. His viewpoint expresses the truth of his life. A twentieth century man experiences himself in much the same way. We are able to understand, then, that Luther's "profound intuitions of the infinite subleties of human egoism, and the dark ferment always at work in the hidden depths of the human soul, anticipate truths

[12] Ibid., p. 31.
[13] Ibid., p. 88.
[14] Ibid., p. 232-3.

which modern psychological science has analytically established."[15]

The theology of Luther was placed in a logical dogmatic form by John Calvin through his *Institutio Christianae Religionis,* appearing in 1536.

The negations of Luther, however, are a source of much confusion. As Luther knew and experienced, man lives in a condition of great paradoxes. Everyone struggles through a tension of opposites or contraries. The temptation is always to narrow down the truth and deny rather than to balance and integrate.

2. *The Catholic Reaction.* A living confrontation with the theology of the first Reformers demanded both a re-thinking and renewal in Catholic theology. Johann Gropper (1503-59) attempted a reconciliation between the conflicting positions in his *Enchiridion* of 1538. Similar efforts were undertaken by Gaspar Contarini (1483-1542) who helped prepare the way for the Council of Trent (1545-1563).

The church itself from the position of its authorities was in a confused state. There were many different opinions being expressed about the meaning and implications of the mystery of God's grace and man's justification. Thomist, Scotist, and Nominalist theories were advocated in the schools. What the Church sought for through the Council of Trent was a coherent group of safe affirmations. These affirmations were obtained through the mediation of scripture, tradition, and the unified thought of Thomas Aquinas.

At the Council specific answers were given but within the general viewpoint of the Catholic community. First, the Council affirmed the fact and habitual presence of original sin among all men. Second, man as a sinner is inwardly and effectively renewed through the Sacrament of Baptism (an effective word and sign), so that one should not speak of a mere external imputation. Third, through justification one is born into a new state—*statum gratiae*—and receives the adoption of sons (Rom. 8.15). Fourth, in every man, even after Baptism, concupiscence remains. Fifth, the final goal of

---

[15] Gordon Rupp, *The Righteousness of God,* New York: Philosophical Library, 1963, p. 167.

justification is eternal life and the glory of God and Christ: *gloria Dei et Christi ac vita aeternae.*

At the Council of Trent, the Catholic community through its representatives gave an answer of faith within a coherent framework of scripture, tradition, and reason. Such an answer is different from a finished and once for all solution. The emphasis is on an unique new life given through the person and activity of Jesus Christ. The answer is opposed to any natural scepticism. What it accomplished was narrow in scope. It rescued Catholic theology from a confusion of Scholastic opinions. It never intended to deny what was true in the affirmations of Luther and the other Reformers.

Basic difficulties remained, however, as Catholics and Protestants confronted each other. Protestants, in general, tended to speak in terms of grace alone: *sola gratia.* Catholics spoke in terms of God's action and man's cooperation. Protestants spoke in terms of faith alone: *sola fide.* Catholics spoke in terms of faith and reason. Protestants spoke in terms of scripture alone: *sola Scriptura.* Catholics spoke in terms of scripture and living tradition.

Each spoke, of course, out of a position of self-understanding. The differences created the united yet separated Christian communities.

The Concept of Grace in Contemporary Theology

1. In the past, as Heidegger has shown, men tended to objectify their manner of knowing. Within such a framework, human language terms referred to ideas or concepts, and these in turn referred to particular objects, a world of things. The term *nature* referred to man, who always existed as a particular object though he shared a common essence with other men. The term *grace* referred to something above man's nature: God himself, some favor of God, some quality or power. God was accepted as a reality, as a pure Act, but considered as an object or thing. God, obviously, must be Pure Act; but he is not a thing or an object. As an object, God appeared to be 'up' in heaven, 'outside' or 'above' man. The term transcendent seemed to refer to some far off Platonic ideal world.

145

But when one turns to actual life and lived experience, he perceives, as did Maurice Blondel (1861-1949), that man is an embodied free act grounded in an immanent yet transcendent free Act or Spirit. From this point of view, man *experiences* himself to be grounded in God. The term *nature* now refers to the human; and the term *grace* now refers to a grounding Presence, the divine. But the term *divine* no longer refers to some far off world, but to what is in man and grounding him. God's Act grounds man's act. In this sense, the human and divine have come together in a living communion. In this perspective grace does not come to be some third thing between God and man. Rather, it is God's creating and loving Act in man offering each human person a shared communion in the divine life.

2. Our life with God is one of shared *freedom*. In this sense freedom and grace belong together. Man experiences himself to be a free, creative, embodied act, grounded in a free, creative Presence. Man's freedom before God is disclosed to him as he exists or lives out his daily life. It is disclosed to him from within himself as he lives out the depths of his total act. His responding acts are those of faith, trust, and love. At the same time we experience God to be free towards us. At times, for one reason or another, we are not aware of his Presence; at other moments, though we are attentive, God appears to both disclose and conceal his loving act. One can only remain open both to the Mystery and the call.

Further, man lives in two worlds: the one within as he makes his inward journey, and the world outside, the world of things and objects. It is always possible for a man to suppress his inward experience. As a free subject, man may lose himself in the world of things. Heidegger, speaking for many others, looks on man as a being thrown into a world of space and time, a world of things. In such a world view, there is little or no place for a living relationship between a holy Presence and reality. Religious experience appears to be an inner psychic process of projected illusions. One has the task to throw himself into a world of the finite. In such a narrow world, one experiences a hopeless care and anxiety. As far as an individual person is concerned, death is the end of everything.

In this context, faith, trust, and love of God and one's neighbor are always free, personal responses. A personal lack of faith and trust likewise are free decisions as one takes his stand in a finite world of things.

3. But here one comes to the problem of *Scripture*, a problem which is often left unnoticed. Faith is always a person's living relation or communion with an experienced, creating Ground and addressing Presence. God's address and call—or God's revelation—always has God as the subject and is given in a living relationship to the human person, either as an individual or in community with his fellow men. Strictly speaking, God's revelation is always an inter-personal address though it may be mediated through human experience, creation, historical events, or words. Even the Incarnation is a personal address and given in direct relation to other human persons. If this is accepted as true, then Scripture cannot be revelation in the strict sense, but is rather a witness to revelation and a representation of a primary spiritual experience.

Scripture, then, is a representation of God's revelation and is, at most, secondary revelation. At some point the principle, *sola Scriptura,* must be questioned. Further, it must be recognized that a set of symbols or words may be defective; though not necessarily the concrete religious experience of a person or the community.

If man's living relationship with a personal Mystery or Thou is taken as primary, then we are able to both notice and critique specific representations set forth in both the Old and New Testaments.

Obviously, of course, the words of Scripture are representations coming from a living faith; yet, they are human words of meaning coming out of a specific world and a set society. God is represented as a king-judge ruling over a slave and servant people. Ideas about God are constructed and balanced by the evidence of the total living experience. In the ancient biblical world, one tended to identify God's voice or word not only with specific laws which came to govern his concrete life, but with everything that happened to him. Man answered in what he did or failed to do.

147

The thinking of our times is characterized by a distinctly different self-understanding. In the depths of our personal solitude we tend to experience a personal, loving Mystery. Usually, in the context of our total experience, we add on the affirmation that God is the grounding creating Act of all things. In this context, we experience God to be a creating, loving Subject. At the same time we experience man to be a personal, free, creative act.

4. It is in this general context that we come to the specific problem of *legal* or forensic justification.

To a large extent, both in the Old and New Testaments, the idea of justice is related to judgment. According to the Hebrew mentality, justice is a justness recognized by a tribunal. He is just who has been declared just.[16] God is the just judge who renders to every man a just judgment about his life and actions. Said another way, God's justice is understood within a particular social context of meaning and given a legalistic construction. The human condition is presented as being in a trial situation and a man's life becomes a conflict between the Creator, who rules as a king-judge, and his creatures. "The wrath of God is revealed from heaven against all ungodliness and wickedness of men who by their wickedness suppress the truth (Rom. 1.18). God as judge both saves and punishes. "By your hard and impenitent heart you are storing up wrath for yourself on the day of wrath when God's righteous judgment will be revealed. For he will render to every man according to his works: to those who by patience in well-doing seek for glory and honor and immortality, he will give eternal life; but for those who are factious and do not obey the truth, but obey wickedness, there will be wrath and fury. There will be tribulation and distress for every human being who does evil, the Jew first and also the Greek, but glory and honor and peace for every one who does good, the Jew first and also the Greek" (Rom. 2. 5-11).

Here the questions arise. If God is a creating and loving Act, if man experiences God to be gracious Presence, how can both the Old and New Testaments speak of God's judgment as not only

---

[16] Cf., J. Guillet, *Themes of the Bible*, Notre Dame, Ind., Fides Press, 1960, p. 24-32; Ernst Kasemann, *Perspectives on Paul*, Philadelphia: Fortress Press 1971, p. 60-78.

saving but condemning and punishing? Does God truly condemn and punish as a strict, legal judge?

In answering the first question, we must recall that the Hebrew mind does experience God to be a creating, loving, or gracious Presence; but this experience is related to a dialectic or play of many diverse factors: light and darkness, truth and error, love and hate, goodness and evil, gain and loss. Within this larger framework we are able to say that man experiences the fact of evil in his relationships to the world, his fellow men, and the holy Mystery. He experiences his own weaknesses and sinfulness. Since man knows himself to be a free subject, he experiences the real possibility of loss and degradation. He is free to accept or reject a higher or lower value, the finite and infinite. Out of this basic human situation man rationalizes and projects his judgments beyond death. Yet, our religious ideas are always associated with our world of space and time and our immediate human interests.

The second question was: Does God condemn and punish as a strict, legal judge? The answer which man gives out of his present self-awareness is: No. God acts in accordance with the nature of his Act. As such he is a creating and loving Presence. But God allows man to be himself and free in his relationships to the world, others, and the immanent Holy. Man condemns himself in and through his acts.

But what is the basis of our judgment? The answer is: We make our judgments about God from the transcendent aspects in man and our living relationships with the Holy. To this the New Testament writings add an historical fact: the death and resurrection of Jesus.

Chapter 8

Man and the Evolutionary Perspective

General Observations

Today modern man lives and thinks within an evolutionary perspective. It is the understanding of man confronting a dynamic yet unified whole. We speak of it as the evolutionary self-consciousness of modern man. It is a viewpoint which comes to the human person "when he is placed fairly and squarely within the framework of phenomenon and appearance."[1]

The universe itself appears to be a dynamic whole, changing and developing continuously. If we look at it from its visible external aspects, it appears to be a physical-chemical whole. One could say that the origin of the universe, as we know it through empirical evidence, was due to an initial explosion of energy which produced vast amounts of hydrogen; and from the energy found in hydrogen particles there developed the universe as we see it. Another possibility is that hydrogen is constantly formed out of the physical properties of energy; and hydrogen becomes the basic unit in the formation of other chemical units.

But how does one explain in a general framework the interior self-awareness found in man? There are obvious developments from simple elements in the physical universe to more complex units. Molecules of hydrogen and helium can interact and give rise to the most complex world of chemical molecules. Further, just as there is a dynamic transformation from atoms to molecules, there also appears to be transformations from molecules of protein and nucleic acid into *living* organisms. Scientists break down viruses into nucleic acid and non-living protein, and then through

[1] Pierre Teilhard de Chardin, *The Phenomenon of Man*, p. 31.

150

a process of synthesis form a new virus. Such experiments suggest the basic factors involved in the development of life forms. One is able to conclude that a unified process of evolution governs the whole universe, from the most simple to the most complex forms. Yet the question remains: How does one explain the transcending self-consciousness found in man while seeking to understand the origin and nature of man from within an evolutionary perspective?

Is evolution a theory, a system or a hypothesis? It is much more: it is a general condition to which all theories, all hypotheses, all systems must bow and which they must satisfy henceforward if they are to be thinkable and true. Evolution is a light illuminating all facts, a curve that all lines must follow.[2]

At the same time, the question of placing man within an evolutionary horizon brings one, sooner or later, to the problem of Christianity. How can one explain within an evolutionary perspective the affirmation made by Christianity that God became man in the person of Jesus Christ? It is extremely difficult for modern man to believe in the existence of a personal or hyper-personal God. We are able to put Jesus in an historical setting and say that he was a man exceptionally conscious of the mystery of the Holy and a prophet of the Holy. But to say that he was and is God-man, seems no more than an empty anthropomorphism.

Again, a third problem arises. How does a Christian live ethically and religiously in an evolutionary perspective and yet find meaning and fullness in being human? How does man reconcile his moral life with the new conditions of a secular world united through scientific means?

The Universe

1. The visible universe, as one man perceives it through empirical evidence, appears to be a unified energy system, that is, a power system manifesting itself in particular wave and quanta forms. The total amount of the material energy in the universe seems to be constant, though its manifestations may change from form to form or from quantum to quantum. In physics, this generally observed

---

[2] Ibid., p. 218.

condition of the universe is known as the law of the conservation of energy, or the first law of thermodynamics. In this frame of reference, the visible universe may be said to be an isolated system. Actual entities in this system exist as ordered *quanta*. Yet there is nothing static, and the universe undergoes a continual process of change. This is a general picture of our physical evolving universe.

Although energy appears to be transferred through specific quanta, the transformation from one form to another form, the available energy in any isolated form or system decreases in the actual process. Every physical form is like a machine. Sooner or later it will break down through an increase of non-available energy dissipated through forms of heat. This is the known phenomenon of the progressive dispersion of energy. In the physical order there is a constant decrease in useable energy in any unified system. We call this the second law of thermodynamics: the law of increasing entropy. An increase in entropy is a decrease in useable energy, bringing with it a breakdown of order. The order of change does not appear to be reversible.

When the second law of thermodynamics is applied to the universe, one comes to the conclusion that sooner or later the whole will "wind-down" and there will result a maximum state of unuseable energy and a maximum deadness, stagnation, chaos.

2. Yet, in a wider coherent unity, things work themselves out differently. The whole reality appears to be a *creative* order. With the rise of complexity in the evolutionary process there comes a leap in quality, the appearance of a deeper more centralized order, the rise of life and consciousness. With the increase of consciousness there comes a leap in energy towards spirit. We are able to perceive that the perfection of evolving reality in our physical universe is found in self-conscious being, in man.

We no longer have in the universe nothing but that heart-breaking entropy, inexorably reducing things (as we are still constantly being told) to their most elementary and most stable forms: but, emerging through and above this rain of ashes, we see a sort of cosmic vortex within which the stuff of the world, by the preferential use of chances, twists and coils upon itself ever more tightly in more complex and more fully centred assemblies.[3]

In this perspective, the evolutionary process is a unified movement, with chance factors working towards greater complexity and higher acts of consciousness. We say there is an evolution of life within matter and the evolution of self-conscious mind within matter. But what we are doing, at least to a large extent, is describing phenomena without explaining it. The question arises: How can we explain the actual evolutionary process if the law of entropy holds true?

3. We are able to say that the evolutionary process is a creative order if a grounding energy or spirit both transcends the created order yet is immanently active in it. Within such a framework God manifests his creative activity through a contrary: creative energy. In this sense there is a play of opposite forces.

The creative order itself is one of process. The general law is one of multiplication of higher acts (internalization).

Within the evolutionary process using the language of Pierre Teilhard de Chardin, we distinguish three movements.

There is, first of all, a cosmic process (cosmogenesis). At times we may think the universe is one of stable or unchanging order. In fact, however, everything in the universe is in process. As far as one considers creative energy in the universe, the basic movement is dipolar: one of moving towards complexity, yet at the same time, one of moving towards an internal unification of act.

There is, secondly, a movement towards organic life (biogenesis). The evidence for the appearance and development of particular living forms is found in the general history of our planet. Chance factors seem to be present. There appear to be groping stages, with lines of advancement going nowhere; yet, there is an ordered finality.

Some writers restrict the word 'evolution' to biological evolution only. This seems to me gratuitous. The universe has had a historical development; so had life, and so had mankind. This historical development did advance

---

[3] Pierre Teilhard de Chardin, *Activation of Energy*, New York: Harcourt Brace, 1970, p. 290.

to life from absence of life, and did ascend to man from non-human ancestors. Although inorganic evolution is due to operation of agencies different from the organic, and human evolution has again causes of its own, life is newer than the universe, and man is newer than life.[4]

There is, thirdly, a living leap or mutation into man (anthropogenesis). "Biological evolution is the middle term of the evolutionary triad—cosmic, biological, and human."[5] The factors of complexity and internalization are at work; yet, there is a transcending mutation in the unifying act. At the same time, the inorganic, organic, and human are subject to different laws.

If the multiple in man is unified in a higher act—the life principle —which transcends matter, the reason for this seems to be a personal, conscious Ground or Center. And it is because of this Ground that one is able to say that all energy or matter has a conscious base.

If the multiple is unified, it is ultimately because it is subject to a pull. If, proceeding from that, we fully analyse this new relation between what is known and what is less known in our experience, we shall become aware of an unexpected aspect in it. Between God who draws and the elements of the world that are drawn, it is clear that the lines of forces are, by nature, in proportion to the psychic quality of the elements: God draws them to the full extent that they are capable of being drawn. This is as much as to say that in the case of man (a centered, that is, a personal being) the descending influx of the divine hyper-center can and must bear the evident character of being centric, that is to say personal.[6]

In such an evolutionary framework, man is able to observe that the perfection of things, or reality, in our physical universe is found in conscious being.

But such a general observation must be unified within the whole of the physical universe. First, the universe is an interacting system and seems to be directed by a transcending energy and, at the same time, an immanent ground. This is God's creative Act, Spirit, or Presence. Second, the universe and everything in it is undergoing a creative transformation. The movement appears to be truly creative and demands, therefore, the influence or causality of God's power; but this power can manifest itself only in a contrary or opposite

---

[4] Th. Dobzhansky, *The Biology of Ultimate Concern*, p. 116.
[5] Ibid., p. 40.
[6] Pierre Teilhard de Chardin, *Activation of Energy*, p. 146.

154

form. This is the process of evolution. Third, because of this, there are two categories of creative activity. There is God's creative activity which is hidden and mysterious; and there is the creative activity found in energy itself. Further, with specific leaps in the quantity of energy, there appear at times leaps in the quality of the unifying acts. Here one may say that God creates in a working harmony with the creative factors present in the universe. As a consequence, every movement is in some sense creative.

The Incarnation: The Problem of Christianity

But how can one explain, within an evolutionary perspective, the affirmation made by Christianity that God became man in the person of Jesus Christ?

1. In the first place, God as a creating Act does not seem to create, multiply, unify, and internalize everything in the universe in the same way. There is some general order present simultaneously with a specific and individual order pertaining to each thing. From the side of God, it appears that he can actualize his creative power in new ways as it pertains to each ordered unit or quantum. From the side of the created object, the order is unique in each, as is the creative process. Each thing is like an individual word: an object of intelligibility. It is as if God were addressing each thing uniquely through an intelligible principle. God seems to create through a mediating word.

Such a conception of the universe was known in antiquity. It appears in the Old Testament when it is said that God creates through Wisdom. It appears in the New Testament when it is said, as in the gospel of John, that God creates everything through the *Logos*. We say today that each quantum of matter seems grounded in mind.

If God is the center of consistency in everything, through a divine intelligible principle (the Word or Logos), if God may be said to speak in creating, then it doesn't sound unreasonable to affirm—or believe—that the perfection of God's centering and speaking can be found in one man who is uniquely God-man.

155

God acts and influences everything in the universe through an expressed Word and Spirit. This is God's extensive influence. In the Incarnation, the action of God in the universe, at one precise point, reaches the depth of perfection. God acts in creation *now* in a divine-human mode. At the same time, God acts in and with the action proper to each created thing. "For the Almighty, therefore, to create is no small matter: it is no picnic, but an adventure, a risk, a battle, to which he commits himself unreservedly."[7]

2. Within an evolutionary perspective, one is able to perceive, then, why God became man in his expressed Word. God *is* engaged, in a manner of wholeness—even using the free power of the human —to bring the multiplication of creation to its goal of a final synthesis.

Created things, as such, have a tendency to fall back into forms of disorder and nothingness. Still, God must work with the conditions of reality at each given moment. Physical and moral evils appear everywhere. In this perspective, God became man to conquer evil and to bring the whole of creation to its final goal.

Seen, however, on the panoramic screen of an evolutive world which we have just erected, the whole picture undergoes a most impressive change. When the Cross is projected upon such a universe, in which struggle against evil is the *sine qua non* of existence, it takes on a new importance and beauty—such, moreover, as are just the most capable of appealing to us. Christ, it is true, is still he who bears the sins of the world; moral evil is in some mysterious way paid for by suffering. But, even more essentially, Christ is he who structurally in himself, and for all of us, overcomes the resistance to unification offered by the multiple, resistance to the rise of spirit inherent in matter. Christ is he who bears the burden, constructionally inevitable, of every sort of creation. He is the symbol and the sign-in-action of progress. The complete and definitive meaning of redemption is no longer only to expiate: it is to surmount and conquer.[8]

3. Third, we must say that the divine actualization (or becoming), implied in the Incarnation, extends to the event and act of the death and resurrection of the God-man.

If the Incarnation may be viewed as God's *actualizing* his Pres-

---

[7] Pierre Teilhard de Chardin, *Christianity and Evolution*, New York: Harcourt Brace, 1969, p. 84-5.
[8] Ibid., p. 85.

ence in a lower manner (kenosis), then, along the same manner of thinking, the Word actualizes the divine Act in a higher and glorified manner through the death and resurrection of Jesus. The human nature is spiritualized or divinized, and in and through a new communication of life from the Word the glorified Jesus engages the whole of creation in a higher creative becoming. "He who descended is he who also ascended far above all the heavens, that he might fill all things" (Eph. 4.9).

Looking at the phenomena of evolution and the reality of the Incarnation, a Christian proclaims—through a community of shared self understanding—that creation is ordered towards the creation of man; the creation of man has been ordered towards the Incarnation of the Word; the God-man, or the risen Lord, orders the whole of creation towards a final goal in God.

The Word became man to live among men, that is, to engage each man in the deepest personal relationship with himself. This interpersonal communion is always subject to a mutual freedom. In an unique way, the risen Lord depends on the free creative activity of each person and the shared activity of human society to render his glorified power effective. "What now has to be done, following the cosmic currents revealed by history, is to confront the future; and that means, now that we have recognized evolution, to drive it further ahead. All the spirit of the earth combining to produce an increase of thinking unity: that is the avenue opening up ahead of us."[9]

Christian Morality

The third problem is: How does a Christian live ethically and religiously in an evolutionary perspective and yet find meaning and fullness in being human? Further, how does man reconcile his moral life with the new conditions of a secular world united through scientific means?

In considering these questions, we must direct our attention to three areas of thought: first, the problem of religious ethical action;

---

[9] Ibid., p. 90.

second, the observation that Christianity is a way of life; and third, the problem of secularization.

1. *The Problem of Religious Ethical Action.* If the universe is evolving with all its parts, so that one must say that man is an evolving essence, how can one form any ordered system of *ought?*

The answer is, in general: any *ought* must follow the nature and actual tendencies of things. From an evolutionary perspective it is possible to say: the act of any existing thing follows the order of creation. In general, a stone acts as a stone should; an animal acts according to its nature and tendencies. Man likewise acts and should act according to his nature: an embodied spirit. Deficiencies and failures happen, or take place, because things do not always act according to a full and well ordered potential.

From an evolutionary perspective, man appears to be grounded in a transcendent yet immanent Power or Presence. Out of his self-awareness, man experiences the intelligibility of such a statement through his power of insight, self-understanding, personal freedom, and responsibility. To be a man, a human person *ought* to act with practical insight, freely, and with responsibility. If one does not act this way, he does not act in a human manner. We can say with Hegel that man learns little or nothing from history; yet the evolutionary aspects associated with human history allow men to perceive the difficulties facing human advancement and the dangers that arise out of human non-advertence.

Traditionally it has been said that since man is a being with intellect and free will, he should act according to his knowledge of the truth and will the good. What is morally good for man is that he should develop and fulfill his nature in being human. At the same time, it is the function of human reason or intellectual insight to both perceive the nature of man's tendencies and to direct them in a free manner. Man's reason must seek to act in a practical manner; for each man, as an evolving historical being, faces, from moment to moment, concrete possibilities.

Ethical and moral action, then, refers to human lived experience. A man acts morally when he lives and develops in a *human manner.*

158

Truth for man is always given in a lived relationship, as he confronts his world, others, and the holy, mysterious *Thou*. Within such a framework, we perceive that we are addressed constantly by the world, by other human persons, and the grounding Mystery. An ordered system of ethics directs these relationships in a human manner as man is addressed from moment to moment. At its depths, ethical life enters into *religious* life, even though one comes to say "No" to God. The religious, as well, survives every period of human scepticism. It is, as we have seen, man's response to a mysterious Presence as he perceives a light shining in darkness.

No moral system can hold together without religion. Or, to put it more precisely, no moral system can live without developing a nimbus of worship. The measure of an ethics is its ability to flower in mysticism. From this point of view, dynamized charity is without a rival.[10]

But we say this facing man's brutal experiences and his miserable practice of religion.

2. *Christianity as a Way of Life.* Christianity is not, strictly speaking, an ideology, or an ordered system of ideas. Rather, it is a community shared *experience* of the loving Presence of God through the Spirit (or dynamic Presence) of the dead and risen Jesus. Most uniquely, it is a conscious religious experience. The church in such a frame of reference is a witness to the existence of Christian faith, a lived reality in men's struggle to be human.

Obviously, such a lived faith is a positive response to the mystery and problem of man based on the perception or sense of a mysterious Presence. Yet, faith is a creative interpretation of the intelligibility of the whole of reality. As man faces a total cosmic evolution, it is an interpretation of human life and self-consciousness in a reference to spiritual values. Christianity is saying that mankind faces a dilemma: either *human* life and man's acts of self-consciousness are delusions or they must be grounded in spirit. Man's total and coherent action becomes the key to the mystery. The evidence associated with personal self-consciousness and freedom are primary.

---

[10] Pierre Teilhard de Chardin, *Activation of Energy*, p. 53-54.

Human thought therefore introduces a new era in the history of nature. But though it is a renewal of life it is not an entirely new life. In its spirituality, as at the apex of a cone, all the productive forces of the past, recognizable though hominized—hunger, love, the sense of struggle, the lust for prey—must appear again. To control these inherited characteristics at a higher level is the task of morality and the secret of 'higher life.'[11]

Much of the joy in being human comes from a self-conscious experience of being a person. Man finds fulfillment in being one's self. One can always confine the task or duty of being human to a narrow egoism. There are moral systems that exult the absolute value of a person's present experience. One can seek to stop or limit the process of evolution with the individual.

Here, however, Christianity senses that the human struggle is *communal*, with the human goal hidden in the future. But what guides and attracts such a communal effort? The Christian both perceives and interprets that the grounding act of all things is a loving Presence. "God is love, and he who abides in love abides in God, and God abides in him" (1 Jn. 4.16).

The phenomenon of Christianity seems to me to have been obscured by the way in which men have tried to define it by certain characteristics which are only accidental or secondary to it. Simply to present the teaching of Christ as an awakening of man to his personal dignity or as a code of purity, gentleness and resignation, or again as the starting point of our western civilization, is to mask its importance and make its success incomprehensible by ignoring its characteristically new content. The essential message of Christ, I should say, is not to be sought in the Sermon on the Mount, not even in the drama of the Cross; it lies wholly in the proclamation of a 'divine fatherhood' or, to translate, in the affirmation that God, a personal being, presents Himself to man as the goal of a personal union. Many times already (and especially at the dawn of the Christian era) the religious groupings of humanity had drawn near to this idea that God, a spirit, could only be reached by spirit. But it is in Christianity alone that the movement achieves its definitive expression and content. The gift of the heart in place of the prostration of the body; communion beyond sacrifice; God as love, and only to be finally reached in love; this is the psychological revolution, and the secret of the triumph of Christianity. Now since this initial illumination the flame has never ceased to grow.[12]

---

[11] Pierre Teilhard de Chardin, *Human Energy*, New York: Harcourt Brace, 1969, p. 28.
[12] Ibid., p. 156-7.

At times Christianity is called a personalist interpretation of the universe. God's creative, loving Act gives rise to the multiplicity of creation with the attending gropings and pains. Yet, multiplicity gives rise to the loving self-consciousness found in man and his creative effort to bring *the whole into communion*. There ought to be an organization of personal human energies into something greater than the human person, through a communal effort. We speak of this today as a morality of movement inclining man towards a creative relationship with the world, with his fellow men, and the pursuit of God.

Yet, at the same time, man faces within himself and his actions the problem of matter and spirit. This problem never disappears but returns in new forms.

3. *The Problem of Secularization.* A final question remains: How can man reconcile his moral life with the new conditions of a secular world? It is relatively easy to answer the question by saying that each man must accept the task of responsibility for his own life and action; or to say that each man must accept the experience and responsibility of his own *humanism*. Such answers may be true, but they are only partially true; for today modern man is caught in a *communal* web of relationships. Technology has united the whole of mankind into a world-wide community. The problems of each man become the problems of all.

We speak of the evolution that has taken place in human society through scientific means as planetary totalization. We observe how this social phenomenon affects the consciousness of almost every man. There is a world-wide sharing of thought and a need for a common humanism. At the same time mankind experiences a process of secularization: an enthusiasm and zest for the world. Human life has become interesting, enjoyable, appetizing. The human community on a world-wide scale seeks to extend the blessings of human life to each man through a dynamic and constructive communal effort.

The problem is one of shared understanding and common action. Today, man in community with his fellow men is engaged

161

in a common task: to give meaning and fulfillment to each man's life, to give him his freedom, and to secure his right for a just life on earth. But what about death? At some point, are we victims of blind energy and chance? Are we prisoners locked into a world of space and time?

As mankind faces the problem of convergence in a technical society, we notice two obvious facts: a) The secularization of human life; and b) man is forced to reflect profoundly upon himself and his life with his fellow men.

a) *The Secularization of human life.* In general, we may think of secularization either as an idea or an historical process.

As an idea or concept, secularization may refer to different levels of human life. It may indicate a man's historical realization of his life in this world. It may mean that religion no longer controls man's ideas, manner of living, or social forms. It may mean that the church no longer controls a man's life. Or, finally, it may suggest that a man lives godlessly. He no longer seeks to live out his life with a conscious relationship to a holy Presence. The result is said to be "secularity": an interpretation of the world without religion, or the freeing of man from the guardianship of religion.

As an historical process, secularization is as old as religion itself. Religion challenges each new generation. Men are always changing their ideas in relation to it as they strive to understand themselves in their world. Specific religious ideas become dead and people seek to emancipate themselves from their control and influence. At times religion misunderstands the meaning and value of the world. People are forced to live in two worlds with conflicting theories. As a consequence, there is a re-action against the old in favor of a new understanding of the world. We immediately think of Buddha attempting to reform Hinduism in the name of human peace, and the indictment published against Socrates in ancient Athens that he did not worship the gods whom the city worshipped.

Secularization as a process of protest against religion is always *ambiguous.* Man is free to protest against truth, goodness, and the holy, for good or bad reasons. A man in misery tends by nature to cry out against the truth and justice he experiences. Truth, goodness, the holy, come to man in this world with a play of opposites. Where there is truth, there is also error; where there is justice there is also injustice; where there is love, there is also hate; where there is the holy, there is also evil. Man, for the most part, must protest from his situation in the world. But to say that the process of secularization is always ambiguous, suggests at the same time that secularity, as a freeing or liberation of man, is a good thing.

From this general frame of reference, we understand today that secularization is a process that works its way out within Christianity. Christianity is embedded in this world and must prove itself to each new generation as a group of people face a concrete history. Often Christianity appears to proclaim that it is in full possession of truth, goodness, and justice. As a consequence, the world must conform. In each historical situation, Christianity rather has the task to be open to the truth and goodness and to serve them while allowing the world to be free in its worldliness. Mankind in secular society senses its own responsibilities.

The world, too, should allow the Church to be what it is: a free community of faith with a common liturgy. Since mankind, as such, only understands itself as a community living in this world, it should be open to the mysterious whole and allow the existence of a possible prophetic light. In this sense, the church constantly questions the world about its understanding of what is true, good, or just. Practical judgments made in the name of the present world can be very narrow and shallow.

A pluralist and 'open' society, which, unlike a 'closed system,' does not merely make room, legally speaking, for a single point of control for all its powers, cannot *a priori* have anything against a community of believers freely and constantly forming itself anew with such an aim, provided only—and this presupposed—that it keeps the 'rules of the game' belonging to such a society. . . .[13]

How the *individual person* lives and reacts in a secular, yet open, society depends largely on his deepest self. He may survive by creating his own illusions. He may act as if he were crazy. He

---

[13] Karl Rahner, *Theological Investigations,* London: Darton, Longman & Todd, 1973, vol. 10, p. 332.

may be completely rational. Or he may question everything in an openness to the world, to his fellow men, to the Mystery we call God.

Of course, what is possible in a pluralist and open society is not possible in a closed system. Here man is constrained or forced to conform to the god and lords of the community.

b) *Dialogue in Technical Society.* As mankind faces the problem of convergence in a technical society, we notice not only the secularization of human life, but the second fact, that man is forced to reflect profoundly upon himself and his life in dialogue with his fellow men. We speak of this living situation as a *compression of socialization* due to the influences of technology.

It is because man reflected as an individual in the past that today he can no longer prevent himself from converging technico-socially upon himself. And, again, it is because he is converging, irresistibly and collectively, upon himself that he is forced to reflect ever more profoundly upon himself and upon all his fellow-men at the same time.[14]

It is because man is able and free to think and reflect that it became possible for him to create human society as such; and through the instrument of technology, to create technological society. And it is because man has created technological society, embracing the whole world, that human society is now compressed together, and all men are forced to reflect and dialogue in a communal manner and more profoundly. No matter how free a person thinks or believes himself to be, he cannot escape the present historical situation which constrains him to think collectively.

The results, from a physical point of view, is like a mass of people caught in a subway train. There is a common experienced agony. Others come too close. One cannot simply be himself, alone, with complete control over his environment. He cannot sit, stand, or fall as he would wish. He is locked in through technology to an unhappy, disagreeable and, at times, hostile collectivity. He is enslaved through the process of mechanization. He can't find air to breathe, food to eat, or water to drink. He becomes extremely

---

[14] Pierre Teilhard de Chardin, *Activation of Energy*, p. 326-7.

nervous and insecure. We hear the cry: "Stop the world. I want to get off."

But if one looks at what has taken place in the evolutionary process, he notices that beyond the mechanization with its forced compression, men have come closer together as conscious beings and are faced with the problems of the whole of mankind. The situation is clarified through the life and service of individual persons.

Apart from the stumbling action of the world, there has been a labour of the individual thinker in man and this has achieved a higher quality and risen to a loftier and clearer atmosphere above the general human thought-levels. Here there has been the work of reason that seeks always after knowledge and strives patiently to find out truth for itself, without bias, without the interference of distorting interests, to study everything, to analyse everything, to know the principles and process of everything. Philosophy, science, learning, the reasoned arts, all the agelong labour of the critical reason in man have been the result of this effort. In the modern era under the impulsion of Science this effort assumed enormous proportions and claimed for a time to examine successfully and lay down finally the true principle and the sufficient rule of process not only for all the activities of Nature, but for all the activities of man.[15]

When we think of men coming together in a shared consciousness, we perceive *the power of man's common reflections*. But man is more than reason, and the "I" is deeper than the human mind. At some point reason leaves the basic human problems untouched. Reason alone never brings persons closer together as human beings. Neither will beautiful words or moral teaching. These, like reason, do not touch the total action of man.

At this juncture, the temptation is to say that the force that gives meaning to man's deepest "I" and to his close relationships with his fellow men is religion. The Christian is tempted further to add the observation that the appearance of Christianity in history meant the appearance of a new humanism, and it is Christianity that will allow modern men to live together in an orderly and just manner.

The strength and power of religion in the world is obvious. The Roman empire used religion to both create and protect public order.

---

[15] Sri Aurobindo, *The Future Evolution of Man*, p. 35.

What is said of Rome may be said of any great state. But, again, religion does not go deep enough. It has to do with man's actions and reactions to his own solitariness, as Whitehead has said, or what a man does with his deepest concerns, as Paul Tillich observed. Often what a man—and the Christian— does in action and in living relationship with his fellow men is narrow-minded, unreasonable, insincere, vicious, and harmful. The needed unifying force is lacking. We have, as Sri Aurobindo wrote, religionism rather than true religion.

It is true in a sense that religion should be the dominant thing in life, its light law, but religion as it should be in its inner nature, its fundamental law of being, a seeking after God, the cult of spirituality, the opening of the deepest life of the soul to the indwelling Godhead, the eternal Omnipresence. On the other hand, it is true that religion when it identifies itself only with a creed, a cult, a Church, a system of ceremonial forms, may well become a retarding force and there may therefore arise a necessity for the human spirit to reject its control over the varied activities of life. There are two aspects of religion, true religion and religionism. True religion is spiritual religion, that which seeks to live in the spirit, in what is beyond the intellect, beyond the aesthetic and ethical and practical being of man, and to inform and govern these members of our being by the higher light and law of the spirit. Religionism, on the contrary, entrenches itself in some narrow pietistic exaltation of the lower members or lays exclusive stress on intellectual dogmas, forms and ceremonies, on some fixed and rigid moral code, on some religio-political, or religio-social system. Not that these things are altogether negligible or that they must be unworthy or unnecessary, or that a spiritual religion need disdain the aid of forms, ceremonies, creeds or systems. On the contrary, they are needed by man because the lower members have to be exalted and raised before they can be fully spiritualized, before they can directly feel the spirit and obey its law. An intellectual formula is often needed by the thinking and reasoning mind, a form or ceremony by the aesthetic temperament or other parts of the infrarational being, a set moral code by man's vital nature in their turn towards the inner life. But these things are aids and supports, not the essence; precisely because they belong to the rational and infra-rational parts, they can be nothing more and, if too blindly insisted on, may even hamper the supra-rational life. Such as they are, they have to be offered to man and used by him, but not to be imposed on him as his sole law by a forced and inflexible domination. In the use of them toleration and free permission of variation is the first rule which should be observed. The spiritual essence of religion is alone the one thing supremely needful, the thing to which we have always to hold and subordinate to it every other element or motive.[16]

What gives fullness to a man's life is not reason, or even religion, but *love*. It is, at this juncture, that Christianity identifies itself as a community experiencing the *loving* Presence of God with its practical demands. "God is love, and he who abides in love abides in God, and God abides in him" (1 Jn. 4.16). From the perspective of evolution, the creation and continuance of the universe and the external manifestation of God's loving union with the whole, confront mankind with two demands: 1) You shall love God; and 2) You shall love your neighbor—friend or enemy—for the love of God. As Chardin observed, Christian charity is both dynamized and universalized, and we are able to perceive that contemporary humanism takes on a Christian attitude.[17]

Finally, once we perceive from an evolutionary perspective that God is a loving Presence entering into a creative union with all things, then we can agree with the contemporary humanist when he affirms that moral values derive their source from human experience.

---

[16] Ibid., p. 44-5.
[17] Pierre Teilhard de Chardin, *Christianity and Evolution*, p. 184-5.

Chapter 9

Hope in Eternal Life

Human Hope

Man is a being who hopes. He experiences some meaning in his world of the present; perceives how it comes to him out of the past; and projects it towards the future. Man, at the same time, is a being ordered towards death. Will the perceived meaning end with death? Or can man hope for a fullness of life beyond death? Man desires a future without illusion. How can he answer as he faces a world in which everything is open to change?

Man answers out of his self-awareness and understanding, but in a dynamic manner: from moment to moment, and in living relationship with his world, others, and the mysterious grounding Power. As man responds, in living confrontation with his fellow men, we are able to observe three aspects: first, a teleology, or man's perception of purpose; second, the Christian experience of God's existence; and third, the absence of God.

1. Teleology

To be human is to seek to surpass what one possesses in the *present*. No man lives, thinks, loves, works or acts without striving to win a personal fullness of life in the future. Why does man live and act in such a manner? Because he is embodied spirit open to the infinite. He must order his life towards the future to establish meaning in the present and to give consistency to his past. We are able to say, as a consequence, that human existence is directed towards the future. Man lives and labors to find fulfillment in the future; but he never possesses the future. In each present he never fully knows if the future will turn out as he hoped or expected.

Why is this? Because a man is a dialectical unit of the infinite and finite. As spirit he is open to the infinite and must seek for the perfection of his personal life in some mysterious future. Yet, he is embodied and caught up in a world of finite necessities.

Because there is present in man a play of the finite and infinite, man's perceived meaning is limited by time. He is aware of meaning, reflects upon it, and understands always in the present, which is given to him from moment to moment. Such an awareness comes to him out of the past and is directed towards the future.

The *past* is a world of happenings or facts. Some things had their act of existing and their time. One can recall these events, however, and bring their intelligibility into the present. In this way man recalls history and understands his own world.

But the destiny of each man is found in the *future*. He must think and plan ahead. Yet, he is never satisfied with any human or social situation. His destiny appears to lie in an order beyond history. With his transcendent openness man seeks to know the whole truth and to possess the perfection of goodness. Since he experiences truth and goodness finitely in his present existence, he tends to hope for the attainment of his personal longing in some future beyond death. He is sceptical about the attainment of an earthly Utopia. In some real way, a better world in which man will be free, peaceful, and possessing a full life is a projected illusion.

Hope, in such a situation where man experiences the play of the finite and infinite within himself, is a consequence of two dynamic factors: man's seeking after a full and perfect life in the future and his experience of meaning and goodness in his personal life. In so far as these aspects are facts, they are not illusionary. Man, as embodied spirit, must hope. He must trust in the possibility of finding a full life in freedom. He must hope as long as he lives or he is not true to himself and his experience.

But what can man hope for? The future is never given as facts of the past or present. One can never picture-out the future as he does with the past. The future, at some point, is beyond the control of man. It is never an event resulting from a development out of a natural or planned necessity.

169

When one looks at the finite in man, as he experiences it in his everyday life, he notices how man is a being in this world. He is embodied and must live, think and act within the limitations of space and time. He creates and finds meaning in this world. He must accept his finitude to be himself. Certainly this finitude is thrust towards the future. But within the order of the finite, man experiences himself to be thrust towards death: *Sein zum Tode*. Death appears to be the final boundary of human life. As Sartre would say, human life has meaning but within the borders of life and death. Death appears to be the revelation of the absurdity of every human expectation.

Since death does not appear on the foundation of our freedom, it can only remove all meaning from life. If I am a waiting for waitings for waiting and if suddenly the object of my final waiting and the one who awaits it are suppressed, the waiting takes on retrospectively the character of absurdity.[1]

Yet, the mystery remains. For man as embodied spirit is a living dialectical tension of the finite and infinite. The tension cannot be resolved on this side of death.

2. *The Christian experience of God's existence.*

Christianity strictly speaking is a manner of living. It is an experience shared in community, an entering into a living relationship with a personal, grounding Presence or Power. From this point of view, Christianity is not a logical system of belief imposed by authority from without, but the experienced reality of a man's life. The source of the understanding lies in the experience of what has been lived through.

In this context, Christianity as a religious community proclaims the good news of God's existence. The spirit of man is experienced to be grounded in a free, creating, and loving Spirit. "In him we live and move and have our being" (Acts 17.28). This Spirit reveals its Presence through the medium of our experience. One may be attentive to the Mystery or ignore it. Yet, as a creating Act, this Spirit gives meaning to man's nature as a dialectic of the finite and infinite. It gives intelligibility to man's nature as embodied spirit,

---

[1] Jean Paul Sartre, *Being and Nothingness*, New York: Philosophical Library, 1956, p. 539.

and life is experienced to have meaning. Our proper response is a living relationship with the Presence while accepting existence as a free responsibility, seeking and expecting an ultimate meaning.

It is this living experience of a grounding Spirit, or God, which allows the Christian to believe and hope that he and all men have been created to live for eternity. One experiences life with God to be eternal life.

The believer perceives and understands, humanly speaking, his destruction (in what has befallen him and in what he has ventured), but he believes. Therefore he does not succumb. He leaves wholly to God, how he is to be helped, but he believes that for God all things are possible. To believe in his own destruction is impossible.[2]

The Christian proclaims, then, that God commends himself to each man as the promise of eternal life and the ultimate meaning of his existence. In this sense, God's creating and loving Presence is offered to everyone as a light and the promise of eternal life.

Christian hope arises out of such an experience, and it is shared in community. Christianity proclaims as good news for all men the content of this consciousness:

1. A living relationship with God as a creating, loving Presence.
2. This experience comes to man in and through an addressing Word. This Word is said to be the dead and risen Jesus.
3. The present experience, clarified through historical events associated with the person and action of Jesus, is understood to be the promise of the future. "We who first hoped in Christ have been destined and appointed to live for the praise of his glory. In him you also, who have heard the word of truth, the gospel of salvation, and have believed in him, were sealed with the promised Holy Spirit, which is the guarantee of our inheritance until we acquire possession of it, to the praise of his glory (Eph. 1. 12-4).
4. This experience comes to man in a living tension of opposites: finite and infinite, freedom and necessity, goodness and evil, hope and fear, life and death.

Such a general perspective makes it clear that, as Teilhard de Chardin perceived, Christianity is a belief and trust in God's creative union with an evolving universe. The creative process is not ab-

---

[2] Soren Kierkegaard, *The Sickness Unto Death*, New York: Doubleday Anchor Book, 1954, p. 172.

sorbed into God. God in creating allows things to be particular realities. Each man takes on a more personal, unique life the deeper he is united to God. As a consequence, man comes to hope for a personal life in God beyond death.

Ultimately God is not alone in the totalized Christian universe (in the pleroma, to use St. Paul's word), but he is all in all of us ('*en pasi panta-theos*'): unity in plurality.[3]

3. *The Absence of God and Despair (Hell)*

Theological anthropology affirms that man is embodied spirit, a unit of a play of opposites, a living dialectic of the finite and infinite. Embodied man is finite. As spirit and grounded in Spirit, man is open to the infinite.

But it is always possible for a man to think or assume that he is grounded in the finite. He can objectify such an attitude through his expressed ideas, words and acts. He can socialize his manner of thinking so that a community of men think the same way. As a consequence, the perception of truth becomes impeded and restricted by the conditions of society. In such a situation one may say that he possesses the light while, actually, he is in the dark. He has restricted man's perception of the truth to the finite; whereas, to be a person he must open his mind to the infinite. In this perspective God's revelation is always a word-event. God addresses each man through the medium of an addressing Word; yet, at the same time, man must be an active and creating subject. He must at every moment be attentive to the grounding Presence and respond with a personal and free activity.

It is said today that modern man lives in a world from which God is absent. Man's attention, interests, and values are restricted to this world. He is guided by an empirical mode of knowing. We say that we live in a world of empiricism and scientific knowledge. Through this mode of knowing man has been able to break or demythologize ancient dualistic symbol pictures (myths) of a God up in heaven and of men down on earth. At the same time, through empirical methods, men have gained a deeper insight into the crea-

---

[3] Teilhard de Chardin, *Christianity and Evolution,* p. 171.

tive activity associated with material energy and have been able to both analyze and control forces which in the past were mysterious. As a result, men have lost a perception of God's continuous activity in nature and history, and they have little or no consciousness of his Presence in their individual life. Contemporary man lives in a world of human created meaning. God not only is experienced as absent, but he appears dead. He does not exist. The term "God" is no more than a projected illusion. What one experiences is his own life in this world.

Empirical man loses, or has lost, conscious awareness of his spirit (that he is a transcendent act) and all perception that he is grounded in Spirit. The visible universe appears to be the whole. His life has no ultimate meaning. As Sartre would say, it is absurd. He must bear its burdens with bitterness. He possesses no lasting hope, only despair.

It is easy, of course, to say that contemporary man must live without God in a world of matter and egoism. This is the fate that has befallen him.

Perhaps man is at *fault* and shares his mistake and sin with his fellow men. He possesses a false and narrow orientation of his spirit. He allows himself to be victimized by the secular viewpoint of others. He walks in darkness because he is not open to the light. He is afraid to take his solitary position. He fails to understand that human knowledge and religious faith are linked with a creative act of the human spirit. God can be degraded by false human ideas. God is not a thing, a being, an object. He is Spirit, a creative Act, Power, or Presence. He grounds man's spirit and offers his Spirit to man's spirit but through a mode of free encounter. Man cannot find this truth in a visible world of things; rather, God's revelation is always Word-Event, or a living communion of the divine and human. Each person to be truly human must face the whole of reality with his spiritual freedom and risk. He must, from moment to moment, be open to the Power that grounds his inmost act. In this context, there must be a personal free awakening and a creative discovery of God's Presence.

173

When man is not open to the Power that grounds him, he becomes confused and lost. He is in despair. *He makes his own hell.*

The determinist or the fatalist is in despair, and in despair he has lost his self, because for him everything is necessary. He is like that king who died of hunger because all food was transformed into gold . . .

The fatalist is in despair. He has lost God, and therefore himself as well; for if he has no God, neither has he a self.[4]

The Resurrection of Jesus and Christian Hope

Ultimately, Christian hope for eternal life rests on the resurrection of Jesus and his risen dynamic Presence. Such a viewpoint was the understanding of the Christian community from the very beginning. "If there is no resurrection of the dead, then Christ has not been raised; if Christ has not been raised, then our preaching is in vain and your faith is in vain" (1 Cor. 15. 13-4). But, immediately, the question arises: How can such a past event become intelligible to me as a human person? The answer is: the past resurrection of Jesus clarifies my present religious experience that I am addressed by a personal Mystery through the medium of a Word; at the same time it clarifies the intelligibility of history within the horizon of the whole of reality. To explain such an affirmation of self-understanding we must look at the past event of the resurrection itself and then perceive what the event manifests.

1. *The Resurrection of Jesus as on historical event.* The Christian community proclaims that the resurrection of Jesus is an event situated in history, or on the borders of history. At the same time, such a past event becomes an experienced Word-event, in so far as it becomes associated with an event of words: either the words of human language or an addressing Word, experienced to be the dead and risen Lord.

There were in past history witnesses to the Resurrection event.

For I delivered to you as of first importance what I also received, that Christ died for our sins in accordance with the scriptures, that he was buried, that he was raised on the third day in accordance with the scrip-

---

4 Kierkegaard, *op. cit.,* p. 173.

tures, and that he appeared to Cephas, then to the twelve. Then he appeared to more than five hundred brethren at one time, most of whom are still alive, though some have fallen asleep. Then he appeared to James, then to all the apostles. Last of all, as to one ultimately born, he appeared also to me (1 Cor. 15.3-8).

Yet the resurrection of Jesus is not reported as a simple historical event taking place within the borders of space and time. It is an event which is both continuous and discontinuous, with ordinary human happenings. If Jesus before his death was true man, he is now in a state of divine glory. If Jesus before his death lived and acted as a servant, he is now the divine Lord, mediating God's creating and loving action. Such an event can only be experienced and interpreted through an encounter of faith. A rigorous analysis of the language statements of the New Testament writings indicate that no human person ever saw the actual event of the resurrection. Rather, what each witnessed was an event associated with a divine addressing Presence of Jesus, a Word-event. As a consequence of this, our perception and understanding of the resurrection rests, likewise, not on a simple historical fact, but on an event as placed within an historical understanding of reality and as each human person with his freedom responds out of a *religious* understanding.

It is crucial, of course, to establish in some real manner that the resurrection of Jesus is an event. If one refuses to accept the resurrection as an historical event, as does Bultmann, because it extends beyond the borders of death and cannot be verified with empirical evidence, he is free to do so. It is not an ordinary historical occurrence. Evidence pertaining to the fact transcends historical verification. One has the responsibility to think and act as he views reality. Yet there was and is *some* evidence associated with the event. There were witnesses who experienced it to be a real happening, though strange and mysterious, disclosing the intelligibility of human history. If it is a real event, traces of evidence will continue to appear.

Such traces must be objectified and socialized. Hence, we come to understand that the experience of the apostolic witnesses, with the perceived evidence, was objectivied in the *language statements* of the New Testament writings. These language statements out of the past, in turn, help us to both perceive and clarify any traces of evidence we discover as we go through life. Further, traces of evidence were also socialized in the resulting *Christian community*, which likewise confronts each of us with its proclaimed idea that Jesus is true God and true man.

In such a perspective, both the language of the New Testament and the proclaimed statements of the Christian community become affirmations of reference. They point to a real event: Jesus has been raised from the dead; he is alive with some relationship with matter; he is Messiah and Lord (Kyrios) mediating God's Presence. Further, if Jesus is the divine Lord, then the Resurrection is an eschatological event. It discloses the final destiny of man. "If Christ is preached as raised from the dead, how can some of you say that there is no resurrection of the dead?" (1. Cor. 15.12).

2. *The Resurrection of Jesus as a revealing of a living Triune God.* Christianity, obviously, looks at the whole of reality from an historical viewpoint. The content of the whole is disclosed in the life, death, and resurrection of Jesus. Jesus is Emmanuel or God with us (Mat. 1. 23; 28.20). Such a perspective is associated with a living experience of the resurrection. "If you confess with your lips and believe in your heart that God raised him from the dead, you will be saved" (Rom. 10.9). The risen Lord manifests the Spirit of God to the world. This Spirit of Jesus is free, active, creating, holy, and loving. Man experiences this Spirit in the intelligibility of creation, history, and himself. God sends the Spirit of his Son, or the risen Lord, into the world. With this sending there is always a new beginning, with a specific freedom pervading the whole.

History in this context is a disclosure in time of the living, free, trinitarian, eternal Act of God. An inner dialectic is revealed. God as God must always affirm his existence and nature. This is the affirming Person of the Father. But in affirming the Godhead, the Father expresses a divine Word—or Son—springing eternally from him in a living dialectic. The Son most truly is not the Father.

176

He is opposite or contrary to the Father. In this sense the Father affirms himself through the opposite. Yet the Father and his Son are united to each other through a dynamic Spirit (or Power) of Love: the Holy Spirit. The living tension between the Father and the Son is resolved because they are joined to each other in an eternal act of Love. The negation is transcended through an act of love. Most truly, God is a dynamic, living, personal Act of love.

In this perspective, creation and human history disclose traces of God's eternal life. God on his part manifests or reveals his eternal act of love, but through a contrary or opposite. Creation is not God. It is opposite to what God is, though God grounds it in a free creative union. Even God's freedom is disclosed in each created thing as it expresses its particular creative activity.

God the Father affirms creation and history through his expressed Word, his opposite or contrary. Any living tension is resolved through the mutual shared Spirit of Love. The perfection of God's creating through his Word, or opposite, would be for God to become man in and through his expressed Word. Such a thought corresponds with the basic Christian affirmation: Jesus Christ is true God and true man. In this perspective, the Incarnation of God in the person of his Word is an historical manifestation of his creating love. Yet God becomes man in and through a tension of an opposite or contrary: in and through a created human being, in and through his Son, not as a ruling Lord, but as a servant with a surrendering love. The person, life, words, and actions of Jesus give evidence of such a manifestation.

As a loving servant of his Father and his fellow men, Jesus submitted himself to suffering and a death as a criminal on a cross. The death expresses the tragedy in the life of one who was uniquely God-man; while the Cross expresses both the depths and the tension of his love for the Father. However, since Jesus is truly God-man, the Father in his loving fidelity to his Son raised him from the dead and glorified him in a higher actualization. Jesus as God-man is alive, glorified and the risen Lord of all things. In and through this risen Lord, the Father is creating and calling all men to himself. Jesus is the first of many brothers. The final destiny of man is disclosed in the resurrection of Jesus.

3. *The Resurrection of Jesus and the meaning of human history.* Today man is sceptical about a unified perception of the intelligibility of history. The energy in matter is associated with a chance factor. Who can really say how things will turn out, either today, tomorrow, or in some future beyond each man's death? Yet, on the other hand, if we consider human history from the perspective of its past events, one is able to place both the call and destiny of each man within a dynamic and free whole. Within the horizon of a living, loving, trinitarian God, the events of history in a strange dialectical manner do make sense. One is able to perceive, darkly, that the call and destiny of each man is to a personal, resurrected life with God. Insight into the origins of the divine life disclose the end. The sign of this end is the resurrection of Jesus. It becomes an anticipation of the end of history. It becomes the definitive disclosure of God's free and future action in creation and human history. Each man on his part must respond and work out his vocation or call freely, in faith, trust, and love.

One particular event, however, cannot disclose fully the end of human history; and this reservation must be applied to the event of the resurrection of Jesus. We merely have traces of evidence. We do not know in any exact manner what has taken place, what is taking place, or what will take place in the resurrected and glorified life of the God-man. The grounding of creation and history lies in a free mystery. The future remains open to the freedom found in every element of the whole. As Christians we proclaim out of a present religious experience, associated with past events, that Jesus is alive, in divine glory and power, mediating God's Spirit. But what this implies with specific objectivity, no one can say. God actualizes his dynamic Presence in and through a contrary and opposite. The disclosure remains veiled and hidden.

4. *The Resurrection of Jesus and engaged human action.* From the situation of human existence in this world, there can be no anticipation without incarnation, there can be no hope without life directed towards the future. At the same time, the risen Lord

in concrete history was a suffering and crucified servant. If he is now the glorified Lord, each human person is a servant and must approach God in imitation of such a Lord. The servant is in no way above the Master. In this context, the risen Lord is disclosed to each man through his committed activities in this world, directing his hopes towards the future and experiencing the trials of human service and suffering.

Man is an incarnate spirit, and to be a human person must incarnate his anticipations in the world. The dialectical paradox is at work in the life of each man. To affirm his transcending act or spirit, he must freely create through the things and values given him in his world. God, as such, has no hands or feet. The risen Lord, though alive and glorified, is dead. He, too, has no hands and feet like we have. The risen Lord must work through his servants.

Man creates the future. No area of human history is excluded: one's personal life, his living relationships to the world, and his encounter with the grounding Mystery. One tends, of course, to think of incarnation in terms of quantity. We come to say that each man must labor to transform history through his human, social, and political actions. Immediate results indicate success. But even here we notice the paradox. In the earthly life of Jesus, his immediate incarnate actions led to his sufferings and death. What had lasting effects was the quality of his committed love to his Father and others. Further, it was God who raised Jesus up. In this context the possibilities of any lasting, ultimate, real achievement rest on the creating and loving power of God. At some point, God must take all of man's successes and failures and transform them. The evidence for this is the resurrection of Jesus.

Again, man is an incarnate spirit who hopes; and there can be no hope without life directed towards the future. Man hopes because he perceives the truth of reality disclosed within himself. Again there is a dialectic at work. In this life the truth is given with its contrary, the untrue, the false, the lie. No thing in this world is exactly as it appears to be. Yet man experiences within himself the need for the whole truth. He searches for truth as he directs his life towards the future. All men are united in this effort and

179

seek to aid each other with a helpful diagnosis. In the darkness all come to a critical point: What can we hope for? The difficulty of the question is increased when all live in an agnostic, passive, or indifferent world.

What gives meaning to Christian hope is the event of the resurrection of Jesus. He is experienced to be the Truth, the Way, the Light. "For this is the will of my Father, that every one who sees the Son and believes in him should have eternal life; and I will raise him up at the last day" (Jn. 6.40). Within this framework of understanding, Christian hope serves the hope of all mankind. One may at any moment freely deny the event of the resurrection of Jesus. Others find themselves in a situation where they hear the event both proclaimed and denied. Yet in such a situation, with its open proclamation of faith, Christianity serves the whole world. It helps each and every man to both analyze and question the hope found in his nature and historical existence. He will be encouraged, perhaps even unconsciously, to face each new moment with a joy and peace which comes from real trust.

But the scandal of each man's death remains before him. It is not removed with the affirmation that Jesus is the risen divine Lord and the sign of man's final destiny. The appearances and experience of death hide such a truth. In this world, the opposite appears to be true. Death appears to be the end of human existence. To speak of a resurrection from the dead seems to be untrue, an error, a lie. But here again a dilectical paradox works its way out. If God discloses the destiny of man in and through the weakness of Jesus, the God-man, who served his Father in the weakness of human nature, so likewise each man must approach the mystery of the risen Lord through similar weaknesses: the darkness of faith, one's sins and failure, one's submission to the mystery of death. In this sense we serve God with our weaknesses rather than with our strength. At the same time, one negates his weaknesses through his service of love. God is love; and he who abides in love abides in God.

This, then, is the deepest burden of human existence: "If any man would come after me, let him deny himself and take up his cross and follow me" (Mk. 8.34).

Conclusion

Man, as a free, personal subject is always brought back to himself and his self-understanding in each present moment. In the world of himself and his shared existence with other men, he confronts the mystery of himself, his life, his death. He repeats each day the same questions: Who am I? What is the meaning of my existence? The questions become more crucial in moments of nonmeaning or as one faces death. Each man must answer the questions for himself, freely and with personal responsibility. Answers are given by each person even when he thinks or assumes that he cannot answer. He answers each moment of his existence through his total action and through his personal relationships to the world, others, and the grounding Mystery.

The Christian likewise asks the same questions each day as he experiences himself to be embodied spirit, open to the infinite and grounded in Spirit. Man is a living tension of opposites, and this tension is manifest in his total action and all his personal relationships. The dialectic is present in his actions of faith, trust, and love.

To be a Christian one lives in a truth of action, in an engaged personal relationship with God through the dead and risen Jesus. His given answers are the expressed truth of faith, hope, and love. He experiences, objectifies and socializes truth within the open horizon of himself, history, and the whole of reality. His living answers point to a personal, eternal life with God beyond death but within the play of opposites. In the darkness of his faith he trusts constantly in the risen Lord as being the sign of the free vocation of every man. Truth in action is to follow a crucified Master.

In a Christian understanding, then, theological anthropology ends with a constant new beginning: a theology of the Cross.

Bibliography

Aurobindo, Sri. *The Future Evolution of Man*. Wheaton, Ill.: Theos. Publ. House, 1974.

Baeck, Leo. *The Essence of Judaism*. New York: Schocken, 1970.

Balthasar, Hans Urs Von. *A Theological Anthropology*. New York: Sheed and Ward, 1967.

Barth, Karl. *Church Dogmatics*. Vol. 3, part 2. Edinburgh: T.&T. Clark, 1960.

Baum, Gregory. *Man Becoming*. New York: Herder & Herder, 1970.

Berdyaev, Nicolas. *The Destiny of Man*. London: Geoffrey Bles, 1948.
————— *The Divine and The Human*. London: Geoffrey Bles, 1949.
————— *The Meaning of History*. London: Geoffrey Bles, 1948.

Berger, Peter. *The Sacred Canopy*. New York: Doubleday, 1969.
————— and Luckmann, Thomas. *The Social Construction of Reality*. New York: Doubleday, 1967.

Bergson, Henri. *Matter and Memory*. New York: MacMillan, 1911.
————— *Mind-Energy*. New York: MacMillan, 1920.

Blondel, Maurice. *L" Action*. Paris: Presses univ. de France, 1950.

Bonhoeffer, Dietrich. *Ethics*. New York: MacMillan, 1964.

Buber, Martin. *Between Man and Man*. London: Kegan Paul, 1947.
————— *Good and Evil*. New York: Scribner, 1953.
————— *I and Thou*, New York: Scribner, 1958.
————— *Kingship of God*. New York: Harper & Row, 1967.
————— *The Knowledge of Man*. New York: Harper & Row, 1966.
————— *Two Types of Faith*. London: Kegan Paul, 1951.

Cassirer, Ernst. *An Essay on Man*. New Haven: Yale Press, 1973.
————— *The Philosophy of Symbolic Forms*. vol. 3. New Haven, Yale Press, 1972.

Cox, Harvey, *The Secular City*, New York: MacMillan, 1965.

Descartes, René. *Philosophical Works*. 2 vols., London: Cambridge U. P., 1912.

Dobzhansky, Theodosius. *The Biology of Ultimate Concern*. New York: New American Library, 1967.

Ebeling, Gerhard. *Word and Faith*. Phila.: Fortress, 1963.

Feuerbach, Ludwig. *The Essence of Christianity*. New York: Harper & Row, 1957.

Fromm, Erich. *Beyond the Chains of Illusion.* New York: Simon & Schuster, 1962.

—— *The Heart of Man.* New York: Harper & Row, 1964.

—— *Man for Himself.* New York: Rinehart, 1947.

—— *Marx's Concept of Man.* New York: Ungar, 1961.

Gehlen, Arnold. *Moral und Hypermoral.* Bonn: Athenäum, 1969.

—— *Der Mensch. Seine Natur und sein Stellung in der Welt.* Bonn: Athenäum, 1952.

Grenzfragen des Glaubens. ed. C. Hörgl and F. Rauh. Einsiedeln: Benziger, 1967.

Groethuysen, Bernard. *Anthropologie philosophique.* Paris: Gallimard, 1952.

Hartshorne, Charles. *Creative Synthesis & Philosophic Method.* La Salle, Ill.: Open Court, 1970.

Hegel, Georg. *Early Theological Writings.* Chicago: Univ. of Chicago Press, 1948.

—— *The Phenomenology of Mind.* New York: Harper & Row, 1967.

Heidegger, Martin, *Existence and Being.* Chicago: Henry Regnery, 1949.

—— *Being and Time.* London: SCM Press, 1962.

—— *An Introduction to Metaphysics.* New Haven: Yale Press, 1959.

Hengstenberg, Hans. *Mensch und Materie.* Stuttgart: W. Kohlhammer, 1965.

—— *Philosophische Anthropologie.* W. Kohlhammer, 1966.

Heschel, Abraham. *God in Search of Man.* New York: Harper and Row, 1966.

—— *Man is not Alone.* New York: Harper and Row, 1966.

Horkheimer, Max, and Adorno, Theodor. *Dialektik der Aufklärung.* Frankfurt am Main: Fischer, 1971.

Jaspers, Karl. *Reason and Existence.* Kegan Paul, 1956.

Jenkins, Daniel. *Beyond Religion.* Phila.: Westminster, 1962.

Kant, Immanuel. *Anthropologie in pragmatischer Hinsicht.* Leipzig: Phil. Bibl. 44, 1798.

—— *A Critique of Pure Reason.* New York: MacMillan, 1927.

—— *Religion within the Boundary of Pure Reason.* Chicago: Open Court, 1934.

Käsemann, Ernst. *Perspectives on Paul.* Phila.: Fortress, 1971.

Kierkegaard, Søren. *The Sickness Unto Death.* New York: Doubleday, 1954.

—— *Training in Christianity.* Princeton: Princeton Press, 1952.

Kolakowski, Leszek. *Der Mensch ohne Alternative.* Munich: R. Piper, 1961.

Lakebrink, Bernhard. *Hegels dialektische Ontologie und die Thomistische Analektik*. Ratingen: A. Henn, 1968.

—— *Klassische Metaphysik*. Freiburg: Rombach, 1967.

Marcel, Gabriel. *The Mystery of Being*. Chicago: Henry Regnery, 1960.

Marcuse, Herbert. *Eros and Civilization*. New York: Random House, 1962.

—— *Negations*. Boston: Beacon Press, 1969.

—— *One-Dimensional Man*. Boston: Beacon Press, 1966.

Moltman, Jürgen. *Mensch. Christliche Anthropologie in den Konflikten der Gegenwart*. Berlin: Kreuz, 1971.

Monod, Jacques. *Le Hasard et la Nécessité*. Paris: Seuil, 1970.

Munby, Denys. *The Idea of Secular Society*. New York: Oxford Univ. Press, 1963.

Mysterium Salutis. Grundriss heilsgeschichtlicher Dogmatik. ed. by Johannes Feiner and Magnus Löhrer. vols. 1-4 (2). Einsiedeln: Benziger, 1965-74.

Nicholas of Cusa. *On Learned Ignorance*. New Haven: Yale Univ. Press, 1962.

Nietzsche, Friedrich. *Basic Writings*. ed. by W. Kaufmann. New York: Modern Library, 1968.

Pannenberg, Wolfhart. *What is Man?* Phila.: Fortress, 1970.

Portmann, Adolf. *Biologische Fragmente zu einer Lehre von Menschen*. Stuttgart: Schwabe, 1969.

Rahner, Karl. *Hearers of the Word*. New York: Herder & Herder, 1969.

—— *Spirit in the World*. New York: Herder & Herder, 1969.

—— *Theological Investigations*. XI vols. London: Darton, Longman, & Todd, 1961-73.

Ricoeur, Paul. *Fallible Man*. Chicago: Henry Regnery, 1967.

—— *Freud and Philosophy*. New Haven: Yale Press, 1970.

Ritschl, Dietrich, *Memory and Hope*. New York: MacMillan, 1967.

Rosenzweig, Franz. *The Star of Redemption*. Boston: Beacon Press, 1972.

Sartre, Jean-Paul. *Being and Nothingness*. New York: Phil. Lib., 1956.

—— *Existentialism and Human Emotions*. New York: Phil. Lib. 1957.

Schaff, Adam. *A Philosophy of Man*. New York: Dell, 1968.

Scheler, Max. *Der Mensch im Weltalter des Ausgleichs*. Berlin: Rothschild, 1929.

—— *Die Formen des Wissens und die Bildung*. Bonn: Cohen, 1925.

—— *Die Stellung des Menschen im Kosmos*. Darmstadt: Reichl, 1928.

—— *Die Wissensformem und die Gesellschaft*. Leipzig: Der Neue Geist Verlag, 1926.

———— *On the Eternal in Man*. London: SCM Press, 1960.

Seeberg, Reinhold. *The History of Doctrines*. Grand Rapids: Baker, 1966.

Seidenberg, R. *Post-Historic Man*. Chapel Hill: Univ. of North Carolina P., 1950.

Smart, Ninian. *The Religious Experience of Mankind*. New York: Scribner, 1969.

———— *The Science of Religion & The Sociology of Knowledge*. Princeton: Princeton Univ. Press, 1973.

Staude, John. *Max Scheler*. New York: MacMillan, 1967.

Teilhard de Chardin, Pierre. *Activation of Energy*. New York: Harcourt Brace, 1970.

———— *Christianity and Evolution*. New York: Harcourt Brace, 1969.

———— *Human Energy*. New York: Harcourt Brace, 1969.

———— *Man's Place in Nature*. New York: Harper & Row, 1966.

———— *The Divine Milieu*. New York: Harper & Row, 1960.

———— *The Phenomenon of Man*. New York: Harper & Row, 1961.

Thielicke, Helmut. *Death and Life*. Phila.: Fortress, 1970.

Tillich, Paul. *Systematic Theology*. 3 vols., Chicago: Univ. of Chicago P., 1951-63.

Wach, J., *Typen religiöser Anthropologie*. Tübingen: Mohr, 1932.

Whitehead, Alfred. *Adventures of Ideas*. New York: MacMillan, 1967.

———— *Concept of Nature*. London: Cambridge Univ. Press, 1971.

———— *Modes of Thought*. New York: MacMillan, 1968.

———— *Process and Reality*. New York: Harper & Row, 1960.

———— *Religion in the Making*. New York: World Press, 1971.

———— *Science and the Modern World*. New York: MacMillan, 1967.

Zimmerlie, Walter. *Was ist der Mensch?* Göttingen, Vandenhoch, 1964.

Index

188

Pelagianism, 138-9.
person (manner of being), 35, 42, 61, 63-4, 72, 78, 109f., 121, 126f.
phenomenology, 1, 5, 13, 37f., 46f., 60f., 150.
philosophy, 24-48, 101, 135f.
physiology, 24, 40.
Plato, 2, 28, 56, 116.
platonism, 54, 135f.
pleasure, 110.
prayer; as life, 7f., 45, 101, 122.
present, 4, 28, 168f.
psychology, 14, 19-20, 24, 40, 41, 45-6.
quanta, 85, 105, 115, 118, 151, 152, 155.
Rahner, Karl, 122-3, 163.
Reformation, 142f.
relationships, 14, 41f., 50, 111, 159.
religion, 45, 51, 116, 119f., 126f., 165f.
resurrection, 55, 61, 171, 174f.
revelation, 66, 126, 147f., 172.
salvation, 54, 57, 77, 81f., 83f.
Sartre, Jean-Paul, 14, 18, 170.
Scheler, Max, 30f., 63, 71.
Scripture; problem of, 147f.
secularization, 68, 69, 161f.
sin, 72, 93f., 100, 173.
Skinner, B. F., 2.
Socrates, 2, 162.
Sophocles, 2.
soul, 54f., 103f., 114, 122.
Stoicism, 135f.
Sum (I am), 92, 108, 109, 111f.
symbols, 27f., 88; Baptism and the Eu-

charist, 134; death and resurrection of Jesus, 100, 102, 134, 156.
Teilhard de Chardin, Pierre, 37-41, 62, 65, 150-167, 171-2.
teleology, 168-170.
Tertullian, 54-5.
theology, 49-70, 129f.
Thucydides, 76.
Tillich, Paul, 166.
Tolstoy, Leo, 70.
Torah, 93.
totality, 39f., 150-167.
tradition, 5, 102, 126f., 135.
traducianism, 55-6.
transcendence, 1, 12, 19, 26, 32, 37, 47-8, 49, 51f., 108f., 154.
Trent; council of, 144-5.
truth, 13, 16-20, 24-27, 28-29, 52, 57, 59, 70, 76-7, 86, 87, 99, 159, 172.
universe; present origin and development, 150-167.
Upanishads, 27.
Valentinian, 54.
values, 35, 94, 121, 167, 170f.
vitalism, 105f.
volo (I will), 109, 110f.
Von Rad, Gerhard, 127-8.
word-event, 50, 66, 172f.
word of God; as revelation, 5, 50, 66, 147f.
Yetzer Hara (evil inclination in man), 93.
Yetzer Tov (good inclination in man), 93.